PamCooks

Favourite Recipes from the Trillium Cooking School

Enjoy!

Pam Collacott

by Pam Collacott

Published by Creative Bound Inc.
(613) 831-3641
on behalf of Trillium Cooking School
R.R.#2 North Gower, ON
K0A 2T0

ISBN 0-921165-70-6
Printed and bound in Canada

Production by Baird, O'Keefe Publishing Inc.,
    Publication Specialists
    Wendy O'Keefe, Designer
    Gail Baird, Managing Editor
Editing by Korin Kealey
Graphics by Brian Collacott
Food photos by Lynn Ball
Portrait photos by Michelle Valberg,
    Valberg Imaging

Canadian Cataloguing in Publication Data

Collacott, Pam, [date]
    PamCooks : favourite recipes from the Trillium Cooking School

Includes index.
Co-published by the Trillium Cooking School
ISBN 0-921165-70-6

    1. Cookery. I. Trillium Cooking School. II Title. III. Title: Pam cooks

TX714.C59 2000   641.5   C00-900677-X

BREAKFAST FOR LEARNING
Canadian Living Foundation

The Breakfast for Learning Canadian Living Foundation is a non-profit charitable organization established in 1992, supporting breakfast programs to relieve child hunger in Canada and to ensure that every child can start the day with an equal opportunity to learn.

The program has three main elements:

- It provides nutrition program grants to partially fund food, equipment and other initial costs.

- It provides a vast array of nutrition education resources to help communities to operate successful nutrition programs and promote nutritious habits and meals.

- It encourages community involvement and shared responsibility through a Community Partners Program with representatives of parents groups, governments, business, volunteer groups and community agencies.

A portion of the proceeds from sales of this book will go directly to the Breakfast for Learning Canadian Living Foundation.

Acknowledgements

This book started to come together about four years ago, shortly after Leanne Cusack and I started to cook together regularly on CJOH-TV. As viewers began to accumulate the recipe sheets we sent to them, they started to ask when we would put their favourites (and mine!) into an easier-to-manage cookbook. Well, it took a while but we finally did it! As is always the case, many people helped to produce this book and I am most grateful for their help.

Read Collacott—The best decision I ever made was to marry you 30+ years ago! You encourage me to reach for the stars, support all of my endeavours with enthusiasm, improve my culinary efforts with your excellent suggestions, and brighten every day with your thoughtfulness and your warm and wonderful sense of humour. I'm so lucky!

Leanne Cusack—The first comment anyone makes about our show is, "You two look like you're having so much fun." That's because we are! I've learned so much from you about how to "do TV" and you inspire me to produce tastier, healthier versions of all my favourite recipes. Your zany sense of humour, quick intelligence and generous and loving nature make working with you not like work at all. Most of all, I appreciate and value your friendship.

Amy and Brian Collacott—My children, who have helped in so many ways. Amy shares my love of cooking and is always ready to test a recipe, pick up a missing ingredient and offer creative suggestions for changing and improving recipes.

Brian, talented artist, produced all of the fabulous and attractive graphics in this book and keeps us laughing with his witty and clever comments and observations. Thanks so much, Sweeties!

Dorothy Searles—Mom, I'm still trying to make soup that's almost as good as yours! Thank you for passing on your love of cooking to me and for generously sharing your recipes, some of which appear in this book.

Elizabeth Baird—My most cherished food friend: we have shared many funny, fabulous food adventures, and hopefully will share many more. Thank you for giving me the nudge that really got me moving on this book, and for always being there with answers to my questions and inspiration for improvement.

"Rellies" and Friends—I'm blessed with many wonderfully supportive relatives and friends: my sisters Deb, Karen, Cathy and Mary Pat, in-laws Enid and Brian Collacott, sister-in-law Susan and all of the spouses, children etc. The "golf girls," all of my friends, and the students who come to the Trillium Cooking School—I couldn't ask for nicer friends or a better crew of booksellers! Warm thanks to all of you.

Korin Kealey—My talented assistant at the cooking school. Thank you for editing this book so well, and for being a constant source of creative and delicious ideas for classes, recipes and marketing. I value your friendship and thank you for all your help and support.

Karen Lewis—Always there behind the scenes when we do a TV show, keeping us honest and on schedule while remaining virtually unflappable! We appreciate your wonderful organizational skills and your quiet and terrific sense of humour.

My Friends At CJOH—Thanks to Garry Bitze, who always finds a few extra seconds when we run a little long, Larry, Ron and all the cameramen who brave the elements to come to the country, Chris and Donnie who beam us back to the city, Maria who prints up all the recipe sheets, Ray who "wired" me into the action, the folks at Reception who field the calls when I'm slow getting the recipes onto my Web page, and to all of the other friendly faces who greet me when I come to the station. My heartiest thanks to all of you!

Lynn Ball—Photographer and friend. Thank you for the mouth-watering food photos that appear on the back cover of this book.

Michelle Valberg and Leslie Anne Barrett— Thanks to Michelle and crew at Valberg Imaging Inc. for the cover photo of me, and warm thanks as well to Leslie Ann, make-up stylist and miracle worker for doing my make-up the day Michelle took the photo—you both made me look better than my best!

Gail, Wendy and Barb at Baird O'Keefe Publishing Inc. and Creative Bound Inc.— It's been 8 years since we worked together on *The Best of New Wave Cooking*, but the years melted away when we started this project. Working with you again has been a friendly, comfortable experience. Thank you for everything.

Food Friends—Members of Cuisine Canada, the Women's Culinary Network of Ottawa and the International Association of Culinary Professionals—so many friends, only an e-mail or phone call away with help, inspiration and support, and with restaurant suggestions when we visit your city! Thanks to all of you!

CJOH "News At Noon" Viewers—This book wouldn't have happened if you hadn't asked for it, and I thank you for your many letters, e-mails, cards and kind and complimentary words.

I hope that this book helps you to create many delicious and memorable meals for your families and friends. Enjoy!

Pam Collacott

Contents

By Popular Demand

Foreword by Elizabeth Baird
Food Director, *Canadian Living* Magazine

That's what prompted Pam Collacott to bring together recipes from her CJOH TV "News at Noon" shows with Leanne Cusack into *PamCooks*. For the last few years, Pam has invited Leanne and the CJOH crew into her kitchen, also the kitchen of the Trillium Cooking School to cook up the kind of delicious recipes Pam makes for her own family and friends. Right from the beginning, viewers clicked with Pam's delectably enthusiastic presentations, and began inquiring about a cookbook of recipes. The requests, complimentary letters and e-mails continue stronger than ever as the show enters its fifth year.

So what makes Pam Collacott's recipes so "in demand"? First and foremost, they taste good. Clearly written and well-tested beforehand, the recipes have a strong emphasis on make-ahead, healthful and family-pleasing flavours. They are not hard to do; in fact, viewers comment on how easy the recipes are to prepare, and to succeed with too. Ingredients are stocked in any local supermarket. These are delicious recipes, viewers tell Pam, they cook again and again—to requests from their families and friends. Everyone knows the kind of recipes I'm talking about. You can always spot them in a cookbook—the pages are spattered and sticky from repeated use and enjoyment.

PamCooks is "by popular demand" for another reason. Pam Collacott is a genuinely wonderful teacher. It showed in her success teaching home economics, it broadened in her classes in the log cabin kitchen of the Trillium Cooking School. But it's with TV that Pam has been able to take teaching people how to cook to a wider audience. That interest in sharing lifeskills with upcoming generations is also what prompted Pam to share proceeds from *PamCooks* with Breakfast for Learning, the community-oriented nutrition programs that provide before-school-breakfasts for kids. From her own experience teaching, and with her own children, Pam is a firm believer that good nutrition is a necessary component of learning.

I know you will enjoy cooking from *PamCooks*. The recipes take you from brunch entertaining, lead you to the barbecue and bread machine, invite you to visit places Pam has enjoyed—Greece and New Orleans, for example—and provide inspiration for all manner of everyday and entertaining occasions. The trademark of a Pam Collacott recipe is the satisfaction it gives to everybody who makes it.

Pam Cooks!

Introduction by Leanne Cusack
Host, CJOH "News at Noon"

I met Pam in a strawberry field. She was getting everyone excited about the delicious berry season, demonstrating new ways to think of this familiar favourite. That's what Pam does, she spreads her genuine enthusiasm and shares her talent and her authentic love of cooking and eating.

We hit it off instantly. We share an understanding that food is an expression of love. It's satisfying to feed people you adore. Pam does more than cook and educate. She is a brilliant food stylist, runs an incredibly popular cooking school (there's a two-year waiting list for her dinner-party classes), writes for Canada's top food publications, and always has time to send her friends home with care packages, or drop off a cake when she knows you're having company. Pam is hospitality! There is always another place at her table. Even when a cooking class is about to descend on her heritage log home, Pam has time to tell a friend who phones that lemon zest will work in a recipe if you don't have lemongrass…

Since that first day in the strawberry field, Pam has become a very important ingredient in our show, the "News at Noon". Every second Monday, she shares her culinary creations with our viewers. Her segment is one of the show's most popular. We have been overwhelmed by the response we get via mail and e-mail. Pam can turn any food from dull to delicious. She can prepare an elegant feast or share very practical, economical tips, like "Five Meals—One Chicken." Her recipes are wholesome but never boring, exotic yet never ostentatious. I'm happy to share a kitchen with Pam. (We also share a sun sign—we are Cancerians—a Catholic upbringing with a pile of sisters and a lifelong appreciation that food doesn't just fill your belly, it fills your heart.)

Cooking for LIVE TV isn't a walk in the park…you have to be organized and unflappable…that's what Pam is. Many times we've told the local volunteer fire department there was no need to panic…ignore the alarm…the BBQ or indoor grill is completely under control!

Like many of our viewers, I have many tattered recipe sheets on Trillium Cooking School letterhead. It's great to now have these faves together in a book.

Over the past five years, Pam has become my food mentor and one of my dearest friends. What more can I say. I'll just lift a glass of Rhubarb Spritzer (page 14) and toast Strawberry Fields Forever!

Grilled Quesadillas

Let everyone assemble their own quesadillas, personalizing them with their unique selection of toppings. A tasty way to start a summer barbecue.

> Flour tortillas, large
> Monterey jack, mozzarella, or Cheddar cheese, shredded
> Green onions, chopped
> Red and green bell peppers, slivered
> Chunky salsa, well drained
> Minced herbs: parsley, cilantro, basil, etc.
> Salsa to garnish

Sprinkle cheese on half of each tortilla to cover. Add your choice of green onion, peppers, drained salsa, herbs, etc. Fold other half of tortilla over. Grill for about 5 minutes per side, or until cheese is melted and tortillas are nicely browned and crisp. Cut into wedges (use a pizza wheel for easy cutting). Serve with more salsa to dip if desired.

Strawberry Sangria Blanca (To Sip with Quesadillas)

In a pitcher combine:

> 1 pint hulled, halved strawberries
> 2 tablespoons *each* sugar, brandy and Grand Marnier

Stir to partially dissolve sugar.

Let stand at room temperature for 1/2 hour.

Add to fruit mixture: 1 bottle dry white wine

Stir to dissolve any remaining sugar. Cover pitcher and refrigerate 4 hours, or until cold.

To serve, place a strawberry in each of 4 glasses. An ice cube may also be added if desired. Fill glasses with wine, then garnish with mint sprigs.

Make It Dinner!

Add strips of grilled chicken breast or beef to the quesadilla toppings for a quick pick-up dinner or meal.

Leanne's comment:
> *Raced home from the show and made these Mexican munchies for guests that night. Yummy and easy....Olé!*

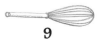

9

Jalapeno Tortilla Pinwheels

Makes 48 pieces

These colourful bites are just the thing to carry to a potluck or cottage party.

1 250 g (8 oz.) package cream cheese, softened
1 1/3 cups shredded sharp Cheddar cheese
1/2 cup sliced black olives
1/4 cup minced green onion
1 clove garlic, minced
1/2 teaspoon ground cumin, or to taste
Jalapeno peppers, slivered, to taste
1 small red pepper, slivered
4 large flour tortillas
Salsa, to garnish

1. In medium mixing bowl, stir together cheeses, olives, green onion, garlic and cumin. Spread 1/4 of the cheese mixture on each tortilla, covering the tortillas completely. Arrange jalapeno and red pepper strips in rows on the tortillas. Roll up tightly like a jelly roll. Wrap in plastic and refrigerate until cold and firm. Can be prepared a day ahead.

2. To serve, slice rolls into bite-sized rounds, 12 to 15 slices per tortilla. Serve plain, or with your favourite salsa to dip.

Leanne's comment:

These are a "pretty" favourite. Sophisticated on one hand and a real hit with kids on the other. You cannot eat just one!

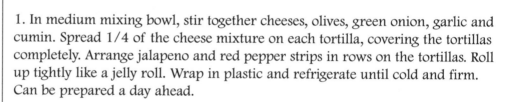
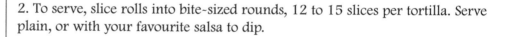

Leanne's Baked Brie

Serves 4 to 6

Keep a package of refrigerated crescent rolls and a small round brie (comes sealed in a tin, so it keeps forever!) in your refrigerator and you'll always be ready for drop-in guests. Leanne put this tasty and attractive appetizer together on the show in about 2 minutes. That's about how long it lasted once it came out of the oven too!

> 1 package refrigerated crescent rolls
> 1/3 cup apricot jam
> 1 small round Brie cheese
> 1 egg white

1. Pinch perforations in crescent roll dough to form two rectangles. Spread half of the jam in the centre of one rectangle; set cheese on jam. Wrap remaining dough around cheese to completely enclose it. Pinch edges to seal.

2. Place cheese on parchment-lined or lightly greased baking sheet. Brush with egg white. Bake in preheated 425° F oven for 15 minutes, or until puffed and nicely browned.

Variation

Substitute your favourite flavour of chutney for the jam.

Time Saver

Cartons of "egg whites only" can be found in the dairy case beside the whole eggs. They are just the thing for recipes that call for only a small amount of whites. Pour what you need out of the carton and avoid having to deal with the rest of the egg.

How to Seed a Tomato

Cut the tomato in half crosswise. Hold the cut surface over a bowl and squeeze the tomato gently until the seeds fall out. Use your fingers to remove any seeds that remain. The tomato is then ready to chop and use in your favourite recipe.

Discourage Double Dipping

Cut vegetables and other items to be dipped into one-bite-sized pieces.

Mexican Chili Dip

Makes 4 cups

This dip is party food at our house. Guests of all ages, from toddlers to seniors, love its spicy flavour and chunky texture. Four cups may seem like a lot, but don't worry about leftovers—there won't be any!

2/3 cup light mayonnaise
2/3 cup light sour cream
2/3 cup plain light yogurt
1/2 package Knorr Leek Soup mix
2 teaspoons chili powder
1/2 teaspoon ground cumin
1 cup shredded Monterey jack or mild Cheddar cheese
1 medium tomato, seeded, diced
1 4-ounce tin diced green chilies (not hot ones)
2 to 3 tablespoons minced jalapeno peppers, to taste
Tortilla chips

In a medium bowl combine mayonnaise, sour cream, yogurt, soup mix, chili powder and cumin until well blended. Stir in cheese, tomato, chilies and jalapenos. Cover and refrigerate 2 hours before serving to blend flavours. Serve with tortilla chips to dip.

Handling Jalapeno Peppers

Always taste jalapenos before adding to a recipe. They can vary in heat level from relatively mild to fiery! Wear rubber gloves while chopping, or be sure to wash hands and scrub under fingernails thoroughly as soon as you are finished. The volatile oils in the peppers can irritate skin and eyes.

Onion Cheese Bites

Makes 2 dozen

You won't believe how good this simple appetizer tastes and how quickly you can make it.

> 3/4 cup grated Parmesan cheese
> 1/2 cup minced green onion
> 1/2 cup light mayonnaise
> Paprika
> Pepper, to taste
> 1 baguette, cut into 24 slices, 3/4-inch thick

Mix first 5 ingredients well. Spread about 1 1/2 teaspoons of mixture on each baguette slice. Place on baking sheet.

Broil 3 to 5 minutes, or until puffed and bubbly. Serve hot.

Make Ahead

Assemble Onion Cheese Bites on a baking tray early in the day, cover with plastic wrap and refrigerate. Pop them under the broiler just as your guests arrive and you'll be munching in no time.

Plan Ahead

Keep a baguette in the freezer (you probably have the other ingredients for Onion Cheese Bites on hand) and you can make these anytime. They taste great for lunch or dinner with a bowl of soup. No green onions? Use finely chopped white onion and add a bit of minced fresh or dried parsley for colour.

Think Stock!

Freeze the wing tips
from this recipe until
you have enough of
them to make a batch
of chicken stock

Leanne's comment:

*You definitely
feel refreshed by
this delightful
drink. It's light.
It's fizzy. It's
a fabulous
alcohol-free
summer drink
and a great use
for all that
rhubarb!*

Peppery Wings

Serves 6 to 8

A tall cool drink, like our Rhubarb Spritzer, is a welcome companion to these spicy nibbles.

> 3 pounds wings
> 2 teaspoons coarse salt
> 1 teaspoon paprika
> 1 teaspoon onion powder
> 1 teaspoon lemon pepper
> 1/4 to 1/2 teaspoon red pepper
> 1/2 teaspoon garlic powder

1. Cut wings into three pieces; discard tips. Wash pieces; pat dry.

2. Mix remaining ingredients. Rub onto wing pieces to coat well. Let stand at room temperature for 30 minutes. Shake off excess seasonings.

3. Grill over hot coals for 8 minutes per side. Serve hot.

Rhubarb Spritzer

Place in medium saucepan:
> 4 cups chopped rhubarb
> 4 cups water

Bring to boil. Cook 10 minutes, or until rhubarb is very tender. Strain liquid through sieve into a pitcher.

Add:
> Juice of 1 lemon
> 1/3 cup orange juice
> 1 cup of sugar, or to taste

Refrigerate until cold. Serve in tall glasses with soda water and ice, garnished with fresh strawberries and mint sprigs.

Pistachio Puffs

Makes 4 dozen

Shelled pistachios are more expensive, so buy them in the shells and shell them in no time while you watch your favourite TV show. Better still, get someone else to shell them!

> 4 green onions, minced
> 1 cup shredded Swiss cheese
> 1/4 cup finely chopped, shelled pistachios
> 3/4 cup light mayonnaise
> 12 slices white or whole wheat bread, crusts removed

1. In medium bowl, combine onions, cheese, pistachios and mayonnaise.

2. Cut each bread slice into four squares. Spread 1 teaspoon of pistachio mixture on each square. Place on baking sheet.

3. Bake in preheated 375° F oven for 15 minutes, or until bread is toasted and mixture puffs slightly.

Shredded Cheese

When you buy more cheese than you can eat before it starts to grow a fuzzy coat, shred the extra cheese and freeze it. Mix several types, then use to make great tasting macaroni and cheese, or use as a topping for casseroles, pizza, quesadillas, omelets or hot cooked vegetables.

Buy and roast rainbow bell peppers in quantity in the summer when they're in season and less expensive. Layer the peeled pepper strips between sheets of waxed paper and freeze. Even after defrosting they retain their fabulous flavour.

Roasted Marinated Red Bell Peppers

Grilling brings out the sweetness in rainbow bell peppers. Don't bother grilling the green ones—they aren't as tasty as the red, orange and yellow ones. Use in this recipe, or on pizza, sandwiches or tossed with hot, cooked pasta and Parmesan cheese.

2 large red, orange or yellow bell peppers
2 tablespoons extra virgin olive oil
2 large cloves garlic, crushed
Minced fresh basil leaves to taste
Freshly ground pepper

1. Wash peppers; leave whole, or cut in half and remove stem and seeds. Place on hot BBQ grill, under broiler or over gas flame, skin side facing flame. Grill until peppers become black on all sides. Place in paper bag until cool enough to handle. If peppers are grilled whole, remove stem, cut peppers in half lengthwise and scrape out seeds. Peel off blackened skin, then cut peppers into strips.

2. Place in bowl with oil, garlic, basil and a sprinkling of pepper. Stir gently to mix. Cover and refrigerate overnight to blend flavours.

3. Spoon pepper mixture onto toasted baguette slices spread with soft goat cheese.

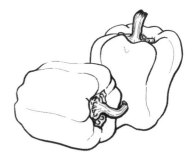

Shrimp and Scallops with Prosciutto

Serve as a starter for special summer feasts. Fresh basil gives these savoury nibbles a fabulous fresh flavour. For an appetizer serving, plan on 4 to 6 pieces per person, depending on size of shrimp and scallops.

Flavoured olive oil (*see below*)
Fresh sea scallops
Large shrimp, shelled and deveined
Prosciutto, thinly sliced
Fresh basil leaves (*optional*)

1. If scallops are larger than bite-sized, cut them in half. Marinate seafood pieces for 1 to 4 hours in olive oil flavoured with crushed garlic, fresh or dried herbs and hot pepper flakes to suit your taste. Wrap each shrimp or scallop in a strip of prosciutto about 1 inch wide. If available, tuck a fresh basil leaf into each piece you wrap. Thread one wrapped shrimp and one scallop onto a short wooden skewer, being sure to stick skewer through prosciutto to prevent it from unwrapping during grilling. Brush again with oil.

2. Grill or broil about 3 minutes per side, or just until cooked through. Transfer to serving platter. Serve hot.

(*photo on back cover*)

Make Ahead

Assemble this appetizer several hours before grilling. Wrap and refrigerate until needed.

Kir Royale

Pour chilled champagne or sparkling white wine into champagne flutes almost to the top. Add about 1/2 ounce of Cassis, a black currant liqueur.

Make Ahead

Prepare Dill Mustard Sauce a day ahead. Several hours before serving, mound salmon on the pumpernickel and place on serving plate. Cover with plastic and refrigerate. Add mustard and garnishes just before serving.

Smoked Salmon with Dill Mustard Sauce

Serves 8 to 10 as an appetizer

This tangy seafood starter turns any party into a special occasion. Add pink peppercorns to the dill garnish at Christmas time.

> 10 ounces thinly sliced smoked salmon
> Thinly sliced pumpernickel bread

Dill Mustard Sauce:
> 8 teaspoons grainy Dijon mustard
> 1/2 teaspoon dry mustard
> 1 teaspoon sugar
> 4 teaspoons vinegar
> 1/4 cup vegetable oil
> 1/2 cup chopped fresh dill

1. Arrange slices of smoked salmon on pumpernickel. Cover and refrigerate.

2. In small bowl, stir together mustards, sugar and vinegar. Whisk in oil. Stir in dill.

3. At serving time, top smoked salmon with a small dollop of sauce. Garnish with dill sprigs.

Leanne's comment:
This is a grand blend of flavours, and pretty too. Irresistible!

Raspberry French Toast

Serves 4

A special treat for the "sweet tooth" in the family, this tastes just like a jelly doughnut!

  4 slices French bread, 1-inch thick
  Raspberry jam
  1/2 cup milk
  2 eggs
  1/2 teaspoon vanilla
  2 tablespoons butter
  Icing sugar

1. Cut bread slices almost all the way through into two slices, but keeping one side of the crust intact. Open the bread and spread raspberry jam in the centre. Close the "pocket".

2. In small bowl, beat together milk, eggs and vanilla with a fork or whisk. Pour this mixture into a pie plate or shallow bowl.

3. Melt butter in large skillet over medium heat. When butter has melted and covers surface of pan, dip both sides of bread slices into the egg mixture, then place slices in skillet. Cook until first side is golden, then turn over with a spatula and cook until the second side is golden.

4. Place cooked Raspberry French Toast on serving plate. Spoon a small amount of icing sugar into a sieve; shake sieve over the toast to dust it lightly with sugar. Serve at once.

Variations

Fill the "pocket" with other things: peanut butter and sliced bananas, chocolate spread and sliced bananas, other jams or jellies, cheese and thinly sliced apple or pear. Use your imagination to create your own unique flavours.

Ham and Egg Strudels

Serves 8

A terrific make-ahead and freeze dish that's perfect for busy holiday brunches. I developed this recipe for a story for *Canadian Living* magazine several years ago.

2 tablespoons butter
2 tablespoons flour
l cup milk
l/2 cup grated sharp Cheddar
l/2 teaspoon salt
Pepper, to taste
6 large eggs
1 cup diced smoked ham (or 6 slices crisply cooked bacon, crumbled)
2 teaspoons minced chives
2 tablespoons minced parsley
1/2 teaspoon dried thyme (*optional*)
8 sheets filo pastry
3 tablespoons Parmesan cheese
Melted butter

1. Melt 2 tablespoons butter on stovetop or in microwave. Stir in flour and slowly whisk in milk. Cook on medium (microwave: Medium, 2 to 3 minutes; whisk often) until thickened. Add Cheddar, salt and pepper and stir until cheese melts. Chill until needed.

2. Scramble eggs with ham or cooked, crumbled bacon, chives, parsley and a bit of salt and pepper, and 1/2 teaspoon dried thyme if desired, until almost cooked. Add egg mixture to cheese sauce.

3. Butter jelly roll pan. Open filo package; keep filo under damp towel to prevent drying out.

4. Brush one sheet of filo lightly with melted butter. Fold in half, long edges together. Brush with butter again. Spoon 1/8 of the egg mixture onto one end of filo, leaving a 1-inch border free of filling. Sprinkle Parmesan on egg. Fold filo edges over egg, then roll up as a jelly roll. Place on buttered baking sheet, seam side down, then brush top with butter. Repeat, making 7 more strudels. Wrap well and refrigerate overnight if desired, or transfer to rigid container, label and freeze for up to 3 weeks. Defrost before baking.

5. Bake at 375° F for 15 to 20 minutes, or until flaky and golden. Let stand 5 minutes before serving.

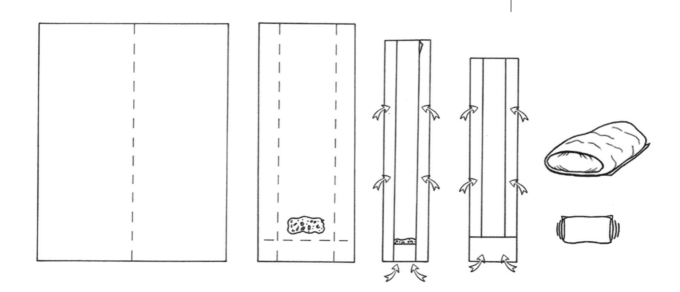

Smoked Salmon Omelet for Two   Serves 2

The perfect entree for a special brunch. Serve with bagels and cream cheese and good strong coffee.

    1/2 cup minced onion or shallots
    1 tablespoon butter
    2 to 3 ounces smoked salmon, chopped
    3 large eggs, beaten
    Salt and pepper
    Fresh dill or parsley sprigs and cherry tomatoes, to garnish

1. In small skillet, sauté onions in butter over low heat until soft but not brown. Turn heat to low. Stir in smoked salmon.

2. Heat large non-stick skillet over medium heat. Brush lightly with butter if desired. Stir a small amount of salt and pepper into eggs. Pour eggs into skillet; tilt pan to coat bottom completely with egg mixture. Cook until egg is completely set, lifting cooked edges of omelet to let uncooked egg slide under omelet onto pan surface.

3. When egg is completely cooked, spoon warm salmon mixture onto one half of omelet. Fold other half over. Slide omelet onto warm serving platter. Garnish with dill or parsley and cherry tomatoes and serve at once.

Old-Fashioned Mashed Potato Rolls

Makes approximately 24

I thought that the recipe for these cloverleaf rolls in my previous cookbook was simple until I developed this even faster, even easier breadmaker version. Enlist the help of your children to shape the tiny dough balls for these fragrant, delicious dinner rolls.

1/2 cup cooked mashed potatoes
1 1/4 cups warm water
3 tablespoons skim milk powder
1/4 cup butter or vegetable oil
1 egg, lightly beaten
4 cups all-purpose or white bread flour
1/3 cup sugar
1 teaspoon salt
2 teaspoons bread machine yeast

1. Measure ingredients into bread machine pan in order given or in order suggested by your manufacturer. Set breadmaker to "dough" setting. Press start.

2. When cycle is completed, remove dough from bread pan; place on floured surface and knead several times. Divide dough into 4 equal balls. Divide each ball into 6 pieces.

3. Divide each of the 24 pieces into 3; roll into balls with lightly floured hands. Place 3 balls of dough into each section of two greased muffin pans. If desired, brush with melted butter or vegetable oil. Cover pans with clean tea towel and let stand to rise in a warm place for 30 to 45 minutes, or until rolls have doubled in size.

4. Bake in preheated 400° F oven for 10 to 12 minutes, or until lightly browned. Serve warm.

Leanne's comment:

Once you get into the habit of making these, you'll always want to throw an extra potato in the pot. These buns taste like the ones your grandmother spent a lifetime perfecting.

"Instant" Mashed Potatoes

When mashed potatoes are called for in a bread recipe, replace 1/2 cup cooked mashed potatoes with 1/3 cup instant mashed potato flakes and 1/3 cup warm water.

Freeze These!

One or two of these rolls, defrosted and warmed in the microwave or oven, will brighten up the most humble bowl of soup or chili.

Focaccia

Makes one focaccia, about 12 x 15 inches

Have one of these assembled and ready to pop into a preheated oven as the first guest rings your doorbell, and 15 minutes later, everyone will be nibbling warm, fragrant focaccia with their drinks.

> 1 recipe of your favourite bread dough, freshly made in bread
>   machine or by hand, or defrosted commercial loaf
> Extra virgin olive oil, plain or spiced (*see Flavoured Garlic Oil,*
>   *see page 67*)
> Chopped fresh herbs, softened chopped sun-dried tomatoes, chopped
>   black olives or thinly sliced fresh tomatoes
> Coarse salt
> Freshly ground pepper
> Parmesan cheese

1. Spread dough as thinly as possible on lightly greased baking sheet. Prick entire surface of dough with a fork.

2. Brush surface with a thin coating of olive oil. Add toppings of choice.

3. Bake in preheated 425° F oven for 10 to 15 minutes, or until nicely browned.

Good and Grainy Bread

Makes 1 loaf

This toothsome loaf makes fabulous grilled cheese sandwiches and excellent toast. Bake in the breadmaker, or choose the "dough" setting and bake in your oven.

Gluten Flour

Add small quantities of gluten flour to recipes that contain mainly low gluten flours such as whole wheat or rye flours. Gluten, a protein found naturally in wheat, helps to make the dough more elastic, allowing it to rise better. Purchase gluten flour in bulk food stores and keep it in an airtight container in the refrigerator.

1 2/3 cups warm water
3 tablespoons skim milk powder
2 tablespoons butter or oil
2 tablespoons honey or maple syrup
2 teaspoons salt
1 1/4 cups whole wheat bread flour
2 1/4 cups all-purpose or white bread flour
1/2 cup 7-grain or red river cereal
1/4 cup quick oats
3 tablespoons natural bran
1 tablespoon flax seed
2 tablespoons gluten flour (*see sidebar*)
1 1/2 teaspoons bread machine yeast

1. Measure ingredients in order given, or in order recommended by the manufacturer of your bread machine.

2. **To bake in breadmaker**: Use "whole grain" setting; press start. Remove from pan as soon as cycle is completed. Cool on rack.

   To bake in regular oven: Choose "dough" setting and remove dough from breadmaker as soon as cycle is complete. Shape dough into a loaf and place in greased loaf pan. Cover with towel; let rise 30 to 45 minutes, or until doubled. Bake in preheated 375° F oven for 45 to 55 minutes, or until top is brown and bottom sounds hollow when tapped. Remove from pan and cool on rack.

Herbed Oatmeal Potato Bread

Makes 1 loaf

This bread made without the herbs is the everyday bread in our house. I think I could assemble the ingredients with my eyes closed, and certainly don't have to look up the recipe any more! I always use the "dough" setting and shape the loaf to bake in the regular oven.

1/2 cup mashed potato (*see tip, page 27*)
1 large egg
1/4 cup vegetable oil
3/4 cup water
1 teaspoon dried herbs: oregano, rosemary, basil or thyme
2 cups all-purpose or white bread flour
1/2 cup whole wheat bread flour
1/2 cup quick cooking oats
1 teaspoon salt
1 tablespoon sugar
1 1/2 teaspoons bread machine yeast
Cornmeal
Egg white and rolled oats (*optional*)

1. Measure ingredients into bread machine pan in order given, or in order required for your breadmaker.

2. **To bake in breadmaker:** choose the "whole grain" setting. Remove loaf from breadmaker as soon as cycle is complete; cool on rack.

   To bake in regular oven: choose "dough" setting. Remove dough at end of cycle. Knead several times on a lightly floured surface, then shape into a large round. Set in place on a lightly greased or parchment-lined baking sheet sprinkled lightly with cornmeal. Cover with clean towel and let rise in a warm place for 30 to 40 minutes, or until doubled in bulk. Brush bread with egg white and sprinkle with oats if desired. Cut several slashes on top with serrated knife.

3. Bake in preheated 350° F oven for 30 to 40 minutes, or until top is brown and bottom sounds hollow when tapped. Cool on a rack.

Oatmeal Molasses Bread

Makes one 1 1/2-pound loaf

This is the breadmaker adaptation of the very first type of bread I baked shortly after Read and I got married. Serve it with homemade baked beans, stew, or your favourite tomato-based soup. It makes terrific sandwiches and toast.

> 1 cup lukewarm water
> 1/4 cup molasses
> 2 tablespoons vegetable oil or melted butter
> 1/2 cup quick oats
> 1 cup whole wheat flour
> 2 cups all-purpose flour
> 1 teaspoon salt
> 1 tablespoon sugar
> 2 teaspoons bread machine yeast

1. Measure ingredients into breadmaker pan in order given or in order recommended for your breadmaker.

2. **To bake in breadmaker:** choose "whole grain" setting, then press start. As soon as bread is baked, remove from pan and cool on rack.

   To bake in regular oven: choose "dough" setting; press start. At end of cycle, remove dough from pan. On lightly floured surface, knead several times to punch dough down. Shape into loaf. Place in greased loaf pan. Brush top lightly with vegetable oil. Cover and let rise in warm place for 30 minutes, or until doubled.

3. Bake in preheated 350° F oven for 45 to 50 minutes, or until top is brown and bottom sounds hollow when tapped. For extra crisp crust, remove loaf from pan and place on rack in oven for 5 minutes more. Cool on rack.

Oatmeal Molasses Buns

Divide dough into 8 equal pieces. Roll into balls. Flatten to desired size. Place on lightly greased baking sheet. Brush lightly with oil. Cover and let rise 30 minutes or until doubled. Bake in preheated 350° F oven for 18 to 20 minutes or until browned. Use for burgers or sandwiches.

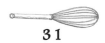

Breadmaker (lower fat) Sticky Buns

Makes 2 dozen

Ask Leanne how many of these she ate the day we made them on the show!

Bread Dough Ingredients:
>   1/2 cup warm water
>   1/2 cup skim milk
>   1/4 cup vegetable oil
>   1 egg
>   3 3/4 cups all-purpose flour
>   1/3 cup sugar
>   1 teaspoon nutmeg
>   3/4 teaspoon salt
>   2 teaspoons bread machine yeast

Other Ingredients:
>   3/4 cup chopped pecans
>   1/3 cup evaporated skim milk
>   1 cup dark brown sugar (*1st amount*)
>   1/3 cup corn syrup
>   2 tablespoons butter
>   2 teaspoons oil
>   1/4 cup dark brown sugar (*2nd amount*)
>   1 tablespoon cinnamon

1. Add bread dough ingredients to breadmaker pan in order recommended by manufacturer. Set to "dough" setting; press start.

2. Sprinkle pecans evenly in two lightly greased 9-inch round cake pans. Set aside.

3. In small saucepan, heat to boiling (stirring constantly) 1/3 cup evaporated skim milk, 1 cup brown sugar, corn syrup and butter. When mixture boils, remove from heat. Slowly pour mixture over pecans in prepared pans. Set aside.

4. When dough is ready, place on lightly floured surface. Punch down and knead lightly to remove air bubbles. Roll into a rectangle, 10 x 24 inches. Brush surface with oil. Combine 1/4 cup brown sugar and cinnamon in small bowl; sprinkle evenly over dough.

5. Beginning with long end, roll up tightly as for jelly roll. Cut into 24 equal rounds. Place 12 rounds cut side up on pecan mixture in each prepared pan. If baking immediately, cover with plastic wrap and let stand at room temperature for 45 minutes, or until doubled. If keeping overnight, cover tightly with plastic wrap and refrigerate up to 24 hours or until doubled. If freezing, wrap tightly, label and freeze for up to 2 weeks. Defrost overnight in refrigerator before baking.

6. To bake (if refrigerated or defrosted), let stand at room temperature for 30 minutes, then bake in preheated 375° F oven for 25 minutes, or until buns are brown and syrup is bubbly.

7. As soon as buns are removed from oven, set a large plate over baking pan and carefully invert to transfer buns and accumulated syrup to plate. Serve warm.

(*photo on back cover*)

Leanne's comment:

Only one word can accurately describe these...IRRESISTIBLE! Pam entrusted me to deliver a pan of these to our audio expert Ray Young. Ray wasn't there when I got back to the station and over the next number of hours the sticky buns disappeared...all 8 eaten. Good thing they were lower fat! I confessed to Pam...told her she should take it as a compliment, and she did. Now all deliveries include advance warning to the recipient, and this story has been stickier than the buns! I've had a hard time living it down.

Substitution

Cooked squash or purchased canned pumpkin can replace the home-cooked pumpkin purée in this recipe.

Arborio Rice

Arborio is a short-grain rice that is used in recipes such as risotto or rice pudding, when a creamy texture is desired. It adds smoothness to this soup.

Autumn Pumpkin Soup

Serves 6

Freeze pumpkin purée in the fall so that you can enjoy this savoury soup all winter long. Just a little bacon gives a smoky depth to the flavour without adding a huge amount of fat.

3/4 cup finely chopped onion
1 large clove garlic, minced
4 slices bacon, finely chopped
2 1/4 cups cooked, puréed pumpkin
3 cups chicken stock
1/4 teaspoon each, salt and pepper
Dash of nutmeg
1/4 cup arborio rice
Cheddar or mozzarella cheese, shredded, to garnish
Salt, pepper and nutmeg, to taste

1. Cook onion, garlic and bacon in large saucepan over medium heat until light brown. Remove bacon mixture from pot; set aside. Discard accumulated pan drippings.

2. Combine pumpkin and stock in same large pot; heat to boiling. Stir in salt, pepper, nutmeg and rice. Cover and cook on low heat for 20 minutes, stirring occasionally, until rice is tender.

3. Stir in bacon mixture; cook for 1 to 2 minutes, until heated through. If too thick, add more stock. Season to taste with salt, pepper and nutmeg if needed. Top each serving with shredded cheese.

Leanne's comment:

This soup makes you want to go for a walk and kick around the autumn leaves. It will leave you feeling warm and satisfied.

Carrot and Potato Vichyssoise   Serves 6 to 8

Serve warm in the winter and cold in the summer for a welcome addition to any meal. Take a thermos of chilled vichyssoise on your next picnic.

>2 tablespoons butter
>1 cup chopped leeks
>3 cups peeled, chopped carrots
>4 cups chicken stock
>2 large potatoes, peeled, diced
>1 1/3 cups milk
>Salt and white pepper, to taste
>Parsley or dill, minced, to garnish

1. In large saucepan, sauté leeks in butter over medium-low heat until soft. Stir in carrots, stock and potatoes; cover and simmer until vegetables are very tender, about 30 minutes.

2. Purée solids in food processor until smooth. Return to saucepan with cooking liquid. Stir in milk and seasonings to taste. Heat just until hot (not boiling) or chill and serve cold. Garnish with parsley or dill.

How to Make Chicken or Turkey Stock

Combine in large stock pot: entire cooked or raw chicken or turkey carcass, including all bones, skin, fat, and meat bits, 1 chopped medium onion, 1 peeled and chopped carrot, 1 chopped stalk celery, a few sprigs of parsley and a few peppercorns. Add enough cold water to cover meat, bones and vegetables. Bring to boil over medium heat. Reduce heat, cover and simmer for about 2 hours. Uncover pot; simmer 1 to 2 hours more, or until liquid is golden and quantity of liquid is reduced a bit.

Pour contents of pot through a colander into a large bowl. Discard solids. Refrigerate stock overnight, or until cold enough that fat forms a solid layer on top of stock. Carefully remove and discard all fat. Stock is now ready to use within 2 or 3 days, or to freeze.

Corn and Crab Chowder

4 generous servings

A soup substantial and satisfying enough to be dinner when served with crusty whole wheat rolls.

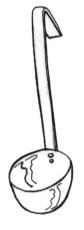

1 tin crabmeat, reserve liquid
2 cups chicken stock
3 slices bacon, finely chopped
1/4 cup minced onion
1/4 cup flour
2 potatoes, peeled, diced
1 cup corn kernels
Worcestershire sauce, to taste
2 cups evaporated skim milk
Salt and pepper, to taste
Parsley, to garnish

1. Drain and flake crab; reserve liquid. In medium saucepan or in microwave, heat crab liquid and chicken stock together until hot. Set aside.

2. In large saucepan, cook bacon and onion together until bacon is crisp. Drain off excess fat. Stir in flour. Slowly whisk in hot stock; stir in potatoes. Cover and cook over medium-low heat for 10 to 15 minutes, until potatoes are tender. Stir often.

3. Stir in corn, Worcestershire sauce and milk. Season with salt and pepper. Garnish with parsley.

Leanne's comment:

Pam and I love sharing soup recipes on the show. Soup is one of those comfort foods that make you feel loved and looked after.

Cream of Turkey Soup with Fresh Herbs

Serves 6 to 8

Use any herbs, meat or poultry and vegetables that you have on hand to create your own versions of this delectable comfort food in a bowl.

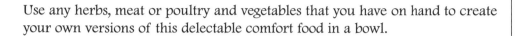

    2 tablespoons butter
    1/2 cup minced onion
    1 large carrot, scrubbed, grated or minced
    1/4 cup flour
    6 cups chicken or turkey stock
    3/4 cup rice
    1 385 mL tin evaporated skim milk (or light cream)
    1/4 cup minced fresh herbs (*choose one or a combination of parsley, tarragon, basil, chives, savory, etc.*)
    1 to 1 1/2 cups chopped, cooked turkey
    3/4 cup leftover mashed potatoes, if available (*if needed, to thicken*)
    Salt and freshly ground pepper, to taste

1. In large saucepan, over medium heat, melt butter and sauté onion and carrot until onion is soft but not brown.

2. Stir in flour. Whisk in stock; heat to boiling. Add rice; turn burner to low and cover pot. Cook for 15 minutes, stirring occasionally, until rice is tender.

3. Stir in evaporated milk, herbs and turkey; add leftover mashed potatoes if soup needs more thickening. Heat soup until very hot but not boiling. Add salt and pepper to taste. Garnish each serving with minced herbs.

Leanne's comment:
      This recipe makes you glad you have turkey leftovers.

Perfect Partners

Onion Cheese
Bites (page 13)
make a perfect
accompaniment
to this and other
creamy soups.

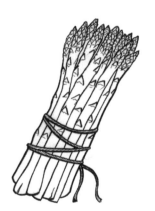

Light Asparagus Vichyssoise   Serves 4 to 6

If you're planning a party to celebrate spring, be sure to include this elegant
yet simple soup. Its pale green colour and light fresh flavour will brighten
winter-weary taste buds. Leanne calls this soup a "spring beauty".

> 1 large leek, chopped (*white and light green part only*)
> 1 large clove garlic, minced
> 1 tablespoon butter
> 4 cups chopped asparagus
> 1 potato, peeled, diced
> 4 cups chicken stock (*or 2 cups stock and 2 cups milk*)
> Salt and pepper, to taste
> Sour cream or Parmesan-flavoured whipped cream, to garnish

1. Sauté leeks, garlic, asparagus and potato in butter in large saucepan until
leeks are tender. Add stock; bring to boil. Lower heat, cover pot and simmer
for 30 to 40 minutes, or until all vegetables are very tender.

2. Purée solids in food processor or blender until smooth. Return to pot with
liquid. Season to taste with salt and pepper. Heat until hot. Serve garnished
with a drizzle of sour cream or a dollop of whipped cream flavoured with
Parmesan cheese.

Minestrone Soup

Serves 8

Whip up a batch of this hearty favourite whenever you find yourself with a surplus of vegetable bits and pieces in your crisper. A variation of "clean the refrigerator" soup with an Italian twist!

2 tablespoons olive oil
2 cloves garlic, minced
1 cup chopped onion
1 cup thinly sliced celery
1 cup thinly sliced carrot
1/2 to 1 cup sliced zucchini
1 cup sliced green beans
4 cups chicken or beef stock
1 28-ounce tin tomatoes, with juice, or 3 1/2 cups seeded,
    chopped, fresh tomatoes
2 tablespoons fresh parsley
1 teaspoon dried basil, or to taste
1 19-ounce tin white beans, drained, rinsed
1/3 cup small shell pasta or broken spaghetti
Freshly ground pepper and salt, to taste
Parmesan cheese, grated

1. In large saucepan, combine oil, garlic, onion, celery and carrot. Sauté over medium heat until vegetables begin to soften. Stir in zucchini, green beans, stock, tomatoes, parsley and basil. Cover and cook over low heat for 20 minutes, or until vegetables are cooked. Stir in beans and pasta; simmer until pasta is cooked, about 10 minutes. Stir occasionally.

2. Season to taste, then serve at once or freeze for future use.

3. Sprinkle each serving with freshly grated Parmesan cheese.

Flavour Tip

Most tomato-based soups, sauces and stews taste better the next day, so whenever possible try to make them a day before you plan to serve them.

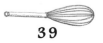

How to Roast Garlic

To roast garlic, trim about 1/4-inch from top of whole head of garlic. Place on square of double foil. Drizzle lightly with olive oil. Seal foil package tightly. Bake in preheated 350° F oven for 1 hour or until garlic is very soft. When cool enough to handle, squeeze soft garlic out of each clove as needed. Store leftovers in refrigerator for several days or in freezer for several weeks.

40

Grilled Tarragon Chicken Baguette with Roasted Garlic Mayonnaise

Serves 4

Grilled Tarragon Chicken is a great dinner entree on its own. Tucked into a warm baguette, it becomes the perfect summer picnic lunch.

Chicken:
4 boneless, skinless chicken breast halves
1/2 cup cider or tarragon vinegar
1 tablespoon fresh (*1 teaspoon dried*) tarragon leaves
1 teaspoon salt
1 large clove garlic, crushed
2 tablespoons olive oil

Remaining Ingredients:
1 baguette, cut lengthwise in half
1/3 cup light mayonnaise
2 to 3 cloves roasted garlic, or to taste

1. Remove fillets from chicken breasts to use for another recipe. Place chicken breasts between two layers of plastic wrap. Pound with rolling pin or wooden mallet until 3/8-inch thick.

2. In a small bowl, stir together vinegar, tarragon, salt, garlic and oil. Place chicken pieces in flat dish large enough to hold them in a single layer. Pour marinade over; turn chicken to coat all sides with marinade. Cover and refrigerate for at least 1 hour, or as long as overnight.

3. Grill for about 5 minutes per side, or until nicely browned and springy to the touch. Cut into pieces that will fit on baguette. Can also be served on crusty rolls.

4. **Roasted Garlic Mayonnaise:** Mash roasted garlic; add enough mashed garlic to light mayonnaise to get the flavour intensity you wish. Add freshly ground pepper to taste. Spread on baguette. Add chicken and other toppings of choice: lettuce or arugula, grilled asparagus, sliced tomatoes or cucumbers, cheese. Cut sandwich into serving-sized pieces. Serve warm.

Mini Calzones

Makes 10 calzones

Let your children help make these for lunch or dinner. Leftovers can be packed for lunch at school the next day.

> 1 package refrigerated biscuits
> Tomato or pizza sauce
> Toppings of choice: chopped peppers, pepperoni, mushrooms,
>   shredded mozzarella cheese, etc.
> Oregano, garlic powder and pepper
> 1 egg, beaten

1. Separate biscuits into 10 rounds. Roll each dough round with a rolling pin on a lightly floured surface until very thin.

2. Spread tomato or pizza sauce in center of biscuit dough round, leaving a rim of dough with no sauce on it. Sprinkle toppings of choice on half of the sauce. Sprinkle lightly with seasonings.

3. Fold dough over filling to make a semicircle, making edges meet. Use the tines of a fork to press edges of dough together securely, and to make several steam vents in top.

4. Use a pastry brush to brush top of calzone with beaten egg. Bake in preheated 375° F oven for 15 minutes, or until calzones are golden brown. Cool slightly before serving.

Muffuletta

Serves 4

This delightful sandwich loaf originated in New Orleans. Take on a picnic to feed the whole gang.

1 8 to 10-inch round loaf of bread
4 ounces Genoa salami
4 ounces smoked ham, thinly sliced
4 ounces provolone or mozzarella cheese, thinly sliced
1 to 2 cups Olive Salad (*see below*)

To assemble sandwich:

1. Cut bread in half crosswise. Layer meats and cheese on bottom half of bread.

2. Top with Olive Salad and the top of the loaf. Press down slightly. Cut sandwich into quarters. Wrap in plastic wrap and refrigerate until serving time.

Leanne's comment:
You'll think you hear a Dixieland jazz band playing when you bite into this yummy Louisiana fare.

Olive Salad

Makes 2 1/2 cups

In medium bowl stir together:

1/2 tablespoon brine from olive jar
1 cup coarsely chopped green olives
3 cloves garlic, minced
1/2 cup marinated cocktail onions
2 stalks celery, thinly sliced
1/4 cup chopped pimientos
1 tablespoon chopped capers
1/2 teaspoon dried oregano
1/2 teaspoon finely ground pepper
1 1/2 tablespoons red wine vinegar
3 tablespoons olive oil

Cover and refrigerate up to 2 weeks.

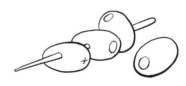

Southwest Quinoa Salad Wraps

Makes about 3 1/2 cups of salad

Many centuries ago the ancient Incas discovered that quinoa was a valuable addition to their diet. It is the grain that comes closest to being a complete protein and can easily be incorporated into your healthy meals. Serve this salad on its own or wrap it in a warm flour tortilla for lunch on the run.

3 tablespoons olive oil
3 tablespoons lime juice
1 clove garlic, crushed
Salt and pepper, to taste
2 cups cooked quinoa
1/3 cup diced cucumber
1/3 cup corn kernels
1 small tomato, seeded, diced (*see How to Seed a Tomato, page 12*)
1/4 cup diced red pepper
1 small ripe avocado, diced
1 green onion, minced
Flour tortillas, warmed

1. Combine oil, lime juice, garlic and a dash of salt and pepper in small bowl; set aside.

2. Gently mix remaining ingredients (except tortillas) together in large bowl. Pour oil mixture over. Toss gently to mix. Taste; adjust seasonings. Spoon along centre of tortillas. Tuck in bottom end; roll up sides.

How to Cook Quinoa

Spread quinoa on a shallow dish; remove any pieces of grit. Rinse well. Cook in double volume of water. Bring to boil. Simmer 15 minutes or until tender and nearly transparent. Drain off any liquid that remains.

Quinoa is pronounced "keen-wa".

Chicken and Vegetable Stir~Fry for Two

Serves 4

This recipe is a good way to use up the last few vegetables in the crisper.

    2 chicken breast halves, cut into bite-sized pieces
    2 tablespoons hoisin sauce
    2 tablespoons soy sauce
    1 teaspoon cornstarch
    1/2 teaspoon sesame oil
    1 to 2 cloves garlic, minced
    Dash salt and pepper
    Pinch of Chinese chili sauce (*optional*)
    5 to 6 cups thinly sliced or chopped vegetables: your choice of
        broccoli, carrots, onion, mushrooms, peppers, celery, bean sprouts,
        green beans or zucchini
    2 tablespoons vegetable or olive oil
    Hot cooked rice or noodles

1. In small glass bowl, stir together chicken, hoisin sauce, soy sauce, cornstarch, sesame oil, garlic, salt and pepper, and chili sauce if using. Set aside.

2. Wash and chop or slice all vegetables. Set aside.

3. Heat oil in large skillet or wok. Stir in vegetables that take longer to cook: carrots, celery, onion, etc. Cook and stir over high heat until vegetables begin to soften. Stir in chicken mixture; cook and stir until chicken is no longer pink. Stir in quick-cooking vegetables; cook and stir until all vegetables are tender-crisp.

4. Spoon mixture over hot cooked rice or noodles.

Chinese Chili Sauce

A very hot and spicy condiment, not to be confused with Canadian-style chili sauce that is more like salsa. Chinese chili sauce should be used sparingly unless you like your food fiery. Indonesian *Sambal Oelek* can replace Chinese chili sauce.

Shopping Tip

Check out the selection of frozen vegetable mixtures in your supermarket. You will find interesting combinations of vegetables in chunks large enough to stir-fry. Saves chopping time when you're caught in a time crunch.

Chicken Fajitas

Serves 2

Crisp colourful vegetables make this "grab and go" meal a winner in our house. It can easily be doubled or tripled when necessary.

    1 chicken breast half, cut into 1/2-inch strips
    Juice of 1/2 lemon
    1 clove garlic, minced
    Dash hot pepper sauce
    Dash each, ground cumin, salt and pepper
    1 medium onion, chopped
    1 tablespoon olive oil
    1 red, 1 green pepper, cut in strips
    Salsa to moisten (*see sidebar*)
    2 large flour tortillas
    Garnishes (your choice of salsa, sour cream, chopped lettuce or
        tomato, shredded Jack or cheddar cheese, guacamole, etc.)

1. Place chicken in small bowl with lemon juice, garlic and seasonings. Stir to mix. Let stand for 15 minutes.

2. Cook onion in oil in large skillet until softened. Stir in chicken and marinade; cook and stir over medium-high heat until chicken is no longer pink. Stir in peppers; cook until hot. Add salsa to taste.

3. Spoon half of chicken mixture in a strip down the centre of a warm flour tortilla. Add toppings of choice. Tuck in bottom of tortilla; roll up. Repeat with second tortilla.

Leanne's comment:

You can't 'fowl-up' this or any of Pam's poultry recipes. They're all easy and delicious.

Fresh Tomato Salsa

Makes about 2 cups of salsa.

Combine in a medium bowl:

2 ripe tomatoes, seeded, diced

1/3 cup chopped green pepper

1 green onion, chopped

1 clove garlic, minced

Fresh basil and cilantro or parsley, chopped

Jalapeno peppers, minced, to taste

Salt and pepper, to taste

Poultry Tips

- When handling raw poultry, be sure to wash the knives, cutting boards and your hands as soon as you finish.

- Store raw poultry in refrigerator, not at room temperature.

- Discard marinade, or boil for 5 minutes before brushing it on poultry as it grills.

- Transfer cooked poultry to a clean platter, never the same one that held the raw poultry, unless of course you wash and dry it first.

Leanne's comment:
Cranberries and maple—how Canadian! Two great tastes combined with Pam's flavourful flare.

46

Maple Cranberry Chicken Breasts

Serves 4

Why not have a dinner party to highlight the arrival of spring? Serve these sweet and savory chicken breasts and celebrate the maple syrup harvest.

> 4 boneless skinless chicken breast halves
> 1/4 cup flour
> Dash of pepper, salt, crumbled rosemary
> 2 teaspoons olive oil
> 1/4 cup minced shallots or onions
> 1 cup sliced fresh mushrooms
> 2 cloves garlic, minced
> 2 teaspoons butter
> 1/2 cup maple syrup
> 2 tablespoons *each*, water and apple cider vinegar
> 1/4 cup dried cranberries
> Parsley and fresh rosemary sprigs, to garnish

1. Flatten chicken breasts between two sheets of plastic wrap. Combine flour and seasonings; coat both sides of chicken pieces with flour mixture; set aside.

2. Heat olive oil in skillet set to medium. Sauté shallots and mushrooms until soft and slightly brown. Add garlic for last minute of cooking time. Remove mixture from pan.

4. Heat butter until bubbly in same skillet on medium-high heat. Quickly brown chicken on both sides.

5. Mix maple syrup with water and vinegar; pour over chicken. Return mushroom mixture to pan. Sprinkle cranberries around chicken. Once syrup mixture begins to boil, set heat to low and simmer, uncovered, until chicken is cooked through (no pink colour remains in centre) and sauce has thickened.

6. To serve, arrange chicken pieces on warm plates or platter, spoon vegetables over and drizzle with sauce. Garnish with parsley and/or rosemary sprigs.

Oven~Fried Parmesan Chicken

Serves 4

This is an easy recipe for children to make. Be sure to wash hands and cutting board well after handling raw poultry.

> 1 egg white
> 2 teaspoons milk
> 1/2 cup grated Parmesan cheese
> 1/4 cup flour
> 1 teaspoon paprika
> Dash salt and pepper
> 4 to 6 servings chicken pieces (*thighs, breasts, drumsticks, wings, etc.*)

1. In small bowl, combine egg white and milk. In second bowl, mix Parmesan, flour, paprika, salt and pepper.

2. Dip chicken pieces in egg mixture, then in Parmesan mixture to coat. Place on lightly greased pie plate, pieces not touching each other. Bake in preheated 350° F oven for 45 to 60 minutes, or until thickest piece of chicken is no longer pink inside, and outside of chicken is brown and crisp.

How to Cut Up a Whole Chicken

1. Choose a broiler chicken that weighs at least 4 pounds. Have a large saucepan ready for trimmings: all skin, bones, etc., that you will not be working with immediately. Sharpen your knife before you begin.
2. Remove wings. To determine where to cut, hold and rotate the wing in your hand, noting where the joint is. Cut through the cartilage at the joint. Cut wing into three pieces at joints. Place wing tips in stock pot. Trim fat from remaining two pieces. Set chicken pieces aside. Place fat in stockpot.
3. Remove legs and thighs in same manner as wings. Remove skin or not, as desired. Separate thigh and drumstick at joint.
4. Remove skin from breast of chicken. Cut breast pieces away from carcass. Place all carcass bones and skin in stock pot. Wrap, label and freeze any chicken pieces you are not immediately using. Make stock, following instructions on page 35.

Curried Turkey and Vegetable Rolls

Serves 4

Use ingredients listed for Curried Turkey and Broccoli Casserole as the base for this recipe.

1. In one bowl mix together turkey and broccoli. Add 1/3 cup slivered red pepper and 1/2 cup sliced mushrooms.

2. In second bowl stir together mayonnaise, soup, milk or water, curry, lemon juice and sherry. Stir 3/4 cup of sauce into turkey mixture.

3. Spoon 1/4 of the turkey mixture into each of 4 small flour tortillas. Roll up filled tortillas and place seam side down in single layer in lightly greased baking dish. Pour remaining sauce over. Sprinkle with cheese.

4. Bake in preheated 400° F oven for 20 to 25 minutes, or until hot and bubbly.

Curried Turkey and Broccoli Casserole

Serves 3 to 4

Thanks to reduced-fat prepared foods such as mayonnaise and cream soups, we can now enjoy a guilt-free version of this quick casserole that has been a favourite of ours for over 30 years. Replace the turkey with cooked, chopped chicken breast if you prefer.

2 cups cooked chopped broccoli
2 cups cooked chopped turkey or chicken breast
1/2 cup light or no-fat mayonnaise
1 tin low-fat cream of chicken soup (*undiluted*)
1/2 cup milk or water
1 teaspoon curry powder (*or more, to taste*)
1 teaspoon lemon juice
2 tablespoons dry sherry
1 cup shredded cheese
Dash of paprika
Hot cooked rice or pasta

1. Spread broccoli in a layer to cover the bottom of an 8-inch casserole dish. If cooking in the microwave, choose a casserole dish that is both microwave-safe and ovenproof. Cover broccoli with turkey.

2. In bowl, stir together mayonnaise, soup, milk or water, curry powder, lemon juice and sherry. Pour over turkey.

3. If baking in the oven, sprinkle cheese and paprika over casserole. Bake at 350° F for 45 minutes, or until hot and bubbly.

If cooking in microwave, do not add cheese before cooking. Cover dish and microwave on High for 8 minutes, or until casserole is hot and bubbly. Sprinkle cheese and paprika over; microwave on High for 30 seconds, or put casserole under broiler until cheese melts and bubbles.

4. Serve over hot cooked rice or pasta.

Turkey and Pesto Pizza

Serves 4

Use small tortillas or pizza shells and let each person create his own "signature" pizza. Read prefers Brie, ripe pears and pesto on his mini pizza. What about you?

> 2 10-inch pizza crusts or large flour tortillas
> 1 cup pesto sauce (*approximately*) (*see page 81*)
> Cooked turkey, thinly sliced
> Toppings of choice: slivered roasted or fresh red peppers, thinly sliced ripe pear, sliced Brie, caramelized onions, crumbled goat cheese, sliced mushrooms, holiday dinner leftovers that you think would taste good on pizza, or other toppings of choice.
> Mozzarella, shredded
> Parmesan cheese, grated

1. Spread a layer of pesto sauce on pizza crust. Add caramelized onions if using. Add other toppings of choice. Sprinkle with mozzarella and Parmesan.

2. Bake in preheated 425° F oven for 10 to 15 minutes, or until crust is brown and cheese is melted and bubbly.

Leanne's comment:

> *If you have leftover turkey or chicken, these little pizzas are the perfect solution. Great flavours...chevrè, pesto, pears and turkey...together!*

Caramelized Onions

Use as a topping for pizza, bruschetta or grilled meats, or tuck into burgers or omelets.

In large skillet sauté:

1 1/2 pounds sliced onions

1/4 cup olive oil

over medium-low heat for 30 to 60 minutes, stirring occasionally, until onions are very soft and sweet. Do not allow them to become overly brown.

Sprinkle with:

1 tablespoon sugar

1 to 2 tablespoons balsamic vinegar

Cook 10 minutes more. Season to taste with salt and pepper.

Fluffy Mashed Potatoes

To make potatoes smooth enough to pipe, beat in milk, as needed, to make them fluffy and easy to spread or pipe onto shepherd's pie.

Turkey Shepherd's Pie

Whenever we have roast turkey or chicken, this ultimate comfort food casserole is always dinner the following night. Use frozen mixed vegetables if there are not enough leftovers.

Leftover turkey, cut into bite-sized pieces
Stuffing
Cooked vegetables (peas, carrots, broccoli, etc.)
Gravy
Fluffy mashed potatoes (*see sidebar*)
Paprika or grated cheese
(*Quantities vary according to how much turkey, stuffing, potatoes, vegetables, gravy, and how many hungry diners, you have!*)

1. Chop turkey into bite-sized pieces. Mix turkey in large bowl with vegetables of choice and enough gravy to moisten. Mix in spoonfuls of stuffing if desired.

2. Spread turkey mixture in a 1 1/2-inch layer in greased baking pan. Spread a layer of mashed potatoes on top, or use a piping bag to pipe potatoes on top of turkey filling. Sprinkle with paprika or grated cheese.

3. Bake in preheated 350° F oven for 30 to 45 minutes, or until hot and bubbly.

Leanne's comment:
A colourful and scrumptious disguise for those leftovers.

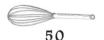

All~Day Pot Roast Dinner

Serves 6

In December when we are outdoors all day running our family's Backwoods Christmas Tree Farm, I put one of these pot roasts into the oven first thing in the morning. A fragrant, warming dinner welcomes us when we come into the house at the end of a long, chilly day. Nice to come home to at the end of a busy day anytime.

1 3-pound boneless pot roast (*cross rib, blade, rump, sirloin tip*)
6 potatoes, peeled (*optional; omit if making mashed potatoes*)
6 large carrots, peeled or scrubbed, cut in half crosswise
6 small cooking onions, peeled
1/2 small rutabaga, peeled, cut in 6 chunks
2 cloves garlic, peeled
2 tablespoons onion soup base
1 teaspoon thyme
1/2 teaspoon rosemary leaves, crumbled
Pepper, to taste
1 cup water, beef stock or tomato juice
2 to 3 tablespoons cornstarch
1/4 cup cold water
Salt and pepper, to taste
Parsley, sprigs or minced, to garnish

1. Brown roast on all sides in large ovenproof Dutch oven over medium heat. Add remaining ingredients except cornstarch, cold water and parsley; cover pot.

2. Transfer to 200° F oven. Cook for 9 to 10 hours, or until meat and vegetables are tender (or at 225° F for 8 hours; or 250° F for 6 hours).

3. Remove meat and vegetables to platter or tray; keep warm in 200° F oven.

4. Add 1 to 2 cups more water or stock if needed to make gravy. Bring liquid to a boil. Dissolve cornstarch in cold water. Stir into boiling liquid. Cook and stir until gravy thickens. Add salt and pepper, to taste.

5. Slice beef; arrange slices and vegetables on warm serving platter. Garnish with parsley before serving.

Shopping Tip

Make friends with your butcher! He will custom cut to suit your needs and suggest the best ways to cook your purchase.

Leanne's comment:
The ultimate comfort food.

Safety Tips for the Grill

- Do not brush meat, fish or poultry with marinade during cooking unless the marinade is first boiled for 5 minutes to cook it completely.

- Have a clean, dry platter ready for the grilled food.

- Never place cooked food on the same platter as the uncooked food without washing the platter first.

- If your marinade has oil in it and drips cause the fire to flare up, have a spray bottle of water handy to quench the flames.

Beef and Vegetable Kebobs

Serves 6 to 8

If you're heading out on a camping trip, freeze the beef cubes in the marinade, then pack the frozen mixture in your cooler. The meat will defrost and be ready to place on skewers by the time you have set up the tent.

Marinade:
1/2 cup vegetable oil
2 tablespoons Dijon mustard
1/2 cup soy sauce
2 teaspoons coarsely cracked pepper
1/4 cup lemon juice
2 cloves garlic, minced
2 tablespoons Worcestershire sauce
1/2 teaspoon dried thyme or rosemary

Other Ingredients:
2 pounds lean top round or sirloin steak, cut into 1-inch cubes
Mushroom caps
Green, red and yellow pepper wedges
Onion pieces

1. Combine marinade ingredients. Place beef in large glass or stainless steel bowl; pour marinade over meat; mix well. Cover and refrigerate for 1 to 2 days, turning meat in marinade occasionally.

2. Thread beef and vegetables alternately onto skewers. Grill over hot coals, to desired degree of doneness. Boil marinade for 5 minutes, if using to brush on kebobs during grilling.

Peppered Steak with Wine Sauce and Mushrooms

Serves 2

An elegant little dinner for two that can be easily doubled or tripled for entertaining.

2 4-ounce beef steaks, either tenderloin or New York strip loin,
    1-inch thick
Crushed peppercorns, to taste
1 tablespoon butter
2 cups sliced mushrooms
1/2 cup chopped onion or leeks
1 clove garlic, minced
1/2 teaspoon dried rosemary
1/2 cup dry red wine
1 cup beef stock

1. Coat both sides of steaks with crushed peppercorns to taste. Cook steaks in hot skillet to desired degree of doneness (use instant-read thermometer to determine this). Transfer steaks to plate and keep warm in 200° F oven.

2. In same skillet, sauté mushrooms, onion, garlic and rosemary in butter until soft and lightly browned. Sprinkle lightly with salt and pepper. Transfer to bowl; keep warm.

3. Pour wine and stock into same skillet; boil gently over medium heat until liquid is reduced to 1/2 cup and has thickened slightly. Return steaks and mushroom mixture to pan; heat through. Serve hot, spooning sauce and mushrooms over steak.

Romantic Dinner for Two

Peppered Steak with Wine Sauce and Mushrooms

Pasta with Toasted Walnuts (page 79)

Garden Tomatoes with Fresh Basil (page 97)

Maple Poached Pears (page 118)

Vegetarian Option: Portobello Burgers

Remove stems from large portobello mushrooms. Clean tops. Brush with same marinade as for Marinated Steak Sandwiches.

Grill over hot coals until nicely browned and tender, about 5 minutes per side.

Serve on crusty rolls topped with grilled onions and roasted garlic mayonnaise, or your choice of condiments.

Marinated Steak Sandwiches with Grilled Onions

The perfect entree for a casual summer supper with friends. Set up the sandwich fixings buffet-style and let everyone help themselves.

> 1 piece of sirloin or tenderized top round, 2 inches thick, or 1 eye of the round roast. Plan on 4 to 6 ounces of beef per person.

Marinade:

> 1/3 cup vegetable oil
> 1/4 cup soya sauce
> Juice of 1 lemon
> 1 1/2 tablespoons Worcestershire sauce
> 1 tablespoon Dijon mustard
> 1 teaspoon coarsely cracked pepper
> 1 clove garlic, minced
> Pinch rosemary and thyme
> Spanish onion sliced 3/4-inch thick (*or Caramelized Onions, see page 49*)
> Dijon mustard
> Crusty rolls

1. Place steak in heavy plastic bag set in bowl. Stir marinade ingredients together; pour into bag. (Note: If you are preparing Portobello Burgers, set aside 2 tablespoons of marinade to brush on mushrooms.) Seal bag and refrigerate 24 to 36 hours, rotating bag occasionally.

2. Before grilling, let meat stand at room temperature for 30 minutes. Grill directly over hot coals just until nicely browned on all sides. Turn off one barbecue burner; place meat on this side of grill. Continue to grill with lid closed until meat reaches desired degree of doneness. Brush with marinade during all but last 10 minutes of grilling. Use meat thermometer to determine doneness: 140° F for rare, 150° F for medium, 160° F for well done.

3. To grill onions: Brush slices with marinade; place on heated side of grill. Cook until onions are tender, carefully turning and brushing with marinade during cooking.

4. To serve: brush crusty rolls with mustard or your choice of spread. Top with thinly sliced steak and grilled onions.

Leanne's comment:
        Fire up the BBQ and enjoy. A real treat to sink your teeth into.

Perfect Partners

Serve with Garden Tomatoes with Fresh Basil, Balsamic Vinegar and Olive Oil
(page 97)

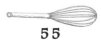

Serving Tip

Serve this casserole with a crisp green salad. In the cold weather months, add a few clementine or navel orange segments to the salad for an extra burst of colour and Vitamin C. Toss with your favourite oil and vinegar dressing.

"Casserole"

Serves 4 to 6

Even though this recipe appeared in my second cookbook, I felt I had to include it here as well. If your family is like mine, this will become one of your favourites. I always double the recipe and freeze half for another day.

1 pound lean ground beef, crumbled
1 cup chopped onion
1 tin cream of tomato soup
2 ounces cream cheese (*1/4 of an 8-ounce [250 g] package*)
1/2 teaspoon salt, or to taste
Pepper, freshly ground, to taste
1 teaspoon Worcestershire sauce
1 cup sliced mushrooms, fresh or canned
1/2 of a 12-ounce (350 g) package egg noodles, cooked and drained
1/2 cup corn flakes or sliced almonds
Paprika, to garnish

1. Crumble beef into a large saucepan. Stir in onion. Cook and stir over medium heat until meat is no longer pink and onion is soft. Add soup, cheese, salt, pepper, Worcestershire sauce and mushrooms; cook and stir until cheese melts and sauce is smooth. Taste and adjust seasonings.

2. Stir in cooked noodles. Pour mixture into an 8-inch round or square baking dish or casserole. Sprinkle with cornflakes or almonds (or a combination of both) and paprika. The casserole can be covered and refrigerated for several hours at this point. Cooking time will be slightly increased if the casserole is cold. It can also be prepared ahead and frozen.

3. Bake casserole at 275° F for 45 minutes or until heated through. Or microwave on High for 10 minutes or until heated through.

French Canadian Tourtière

Serves 6

This is a Christmas Eve tradition I wouldn't dream of changing. You can use any combination of ground beef, veal or pork in this recipe, but be sure to keep the total weight of meat at 1 1/2 pounds.

No-Fail Pastry:
> 2/3 cup shortening or lard
> 1/3 cup boiling water
> 2 cups cake and pastry flour
> 3/4 teaspoon salt

Filling:
> 3/4 pound each, lean ground beef and veal
> 1 medium onion, finely chopped
> 1/3 cup boiling water
> 1 clove garlic, minced
> 1 to 1 1/2 teaspoons salt
> 1/4 teaspoon pepper
> Sage, to taste
> Cinnamon and nutmeg, to taste
> 2 medium potatoes, cooked and mashed (or enough instant mashed potatoes to thicken)

1. **Pastry:** In medium bowl, whisk shortening and boiling water together until smooth. Add flour and salt; mix well with a fork. Dough will be sticky. Cover and refrigerate for 30 to 60 minutes before rolling.

2. **Filling:** In large saucepan stir together beef, veal, onion, water, garlic, salt and spices. Cook over medium heat until no pink colour remains and most of the liquid evaporates. Cover and cook for 45 minutes. Stir in mashed potatoes. Cool completely.

3. Preheat oven to 450° F. Line a deep 9-inch pie plate with pastry. Fill with cooled meat mixture. Add top crust. Seal and flute edges. Cut steam vent in top. Brush top with milk or cream. Bake at 450° F for 15 minutes. Lower oven temperature to 350° F; bake for 30 to 40 minutes more, or until crust is golden. Cool completely before freezing.

Serving Suggestion

Serve Tourtière with mustard, ketchup, chili sauce, or your favourite condiments.

Christmas Eve Menu

Smoked Salmon with Dill Mustard Sauce (page 18)

French Canadian Tourtière

Avocado and Clementine Salad (page 94)

Lemon Meringues (page 114)

Assorted Christmas Cookies

Mexican Meatloaf

Serves 6

A southwestern take on a traditional comfort food favourite. Looks and tastes terrific.

Leanne's comment:
The most satisfying meatloaf I've ever tasted. This has ooomph!

Comfort Food Menu

Mexican Meatloaf

Garlic Mashed Potatoes
(page 87)

Green Beans with
Mustard Cream Sauce
(page 84)

Greek Salad
(page 98)

Chocolate Banana
Trifle (page 112)

Meat Mixture:
1 1/2 pounds lean ground beef
1 cup dry breadcrumbs (*you can replace some of the breadcrumbs with oat bran or rolled oats, if desired*)
2 eggs
1/2 cup salsa
1/2 cup finely chopped onion
1 teaspoon each, salt and minced fresh garlic
1/2 teaspoon each, ground cumin and chili powder
1/4 teaspoon pepper
Dash hot pepper sauce

Filling:
1 tablespoon oil
1 large clove garlic, minced
1/2 cup finely chopped onion
1/2 cup each finely chopped red, green and yellow bell peppers
Jalapenos, finely chopped, to taste
1/2 teaspoon each oregano and cumin
Salt and pepper, to taste
1 1/2 cups shredded Monterey jack, Cheddar or mozzarella cheese

1. In large bowl, mix all meat mixture ingredients. Refrigerate until needed.

2. In large skillet sauté garlic, onion and peppers, including jalapenos, in oil until soft but not brown. Add seasonings. Set aside to cool.

3. **To assemble:** On plastic wrap or foil, spread meat mixture into a rectangle 9 x 12 inches. Spread pepper filling evenly over meat. Top with cheese. Starting at one short end, roll up tightly, using the plastic wrap to help you roll. Pinch ends to seal. Place roll seam side down in a loaf pan. Bake in preheated 350° F oven for 1 to 1 1/4 hours, or until meat thermometer inserted into centre of roll registers 150° F. Let stand 10 minutes before slicing.

Grilled Butterflied Leg of Lamb

A fabulous meal to celebrate Easter, May 24th weekend, Canada Day, your birthday or any time you want to treat friends and family. Ask your butcher to "butterfly" the lamb for you. Makes 2 to 3 servings per pound.

      1 leg of lamb, butterflied
      1 cup dry red wine
      3/4 cup soy sauce
      4 cloves garlic, crushed
      1/2 cup chopped fresh mint
      2 tablespoons fresh rosemary
      1 tablespoon pepper
      1/4 cup oil

1. Place lamb in shallow pan. Combine remaining ingredients and pour over lamb, coating both sides with the mixture. Cover and refrigerate for 6 to 36 hours, turning frequently. Take lamb out of refrigerator 30 minutes before you plan to start grilling.

2. Grill over hot coals until browned on all sides. Turn off burner on one side of barbecue; place lamb on the unheated side of grill. Close the lid of the barbecue during grilling. Baste frequently with marinade. Cook to desired degree of doneness (140° F on meat thermometer for rare). Slice thinly. Serve with Mint Sauce.

Mint Sauce
Makes 1 cup

Heat together in small saucepan:

      1 cup white vinegar
      1/2 cup sugar
      1 1/2 cups chopped fresh mint leaves

Heat to boiling, stirring until sugar dissolves.

Let stand 1 hour before serving. Store in refrigerator.

Canada Day Barbecue Menu

Grilled Quesadillas
(page 9)

Grilled Butterflied Leg of Lamb

Foil-Roasted New Potatoes (page 87)

Black Bean and Corn Salad (page 95)

Strawberry Ice Cream (page 119)

Big Batch Brownies (page 100)

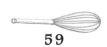

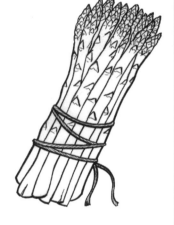

Cheddar Gougère with Ham and Spring Vegetables

Serves 4 to 6

You will love the way this dish looks and tastes, a choux pastry ring studded with melting Cheddar, surrounding a colourful ham and vegetable filling. Perfect for brunch, lunch or a light supper.

Filling:

> 2 tablespoons butter
> 1/2 cup chopped leeks or onion
> 3/4 cup sliced mushrooms
> 1/2 cup sliced asparagus or snow peas
> 1 1/2 tablespoons flour
> 1 cup chicken stock
> 1 cup slivered or diced ham
> 1 ripe tomato, seeded, chopped
> Salt and pepper to taste
> Parsley, minced, to garnish

Gougère:

> 1 cup water
> 1/2 cup butter
> 1 cup all-purpose flour
> Dash salt and pepper
> 3 to 4 eggs
> 1/2 cup diced old Cheddar cheese
> 2 tablespoons shredded Cheddar to garnish

1. **Filling:** In large saucepan sauté leeks mushrooms and asparagus in butter until tender-crisp. Stir in flour. Gradually add stock, stirring constantly, until slightly thickened. Stir in ham, tomato and seasonings to taste. Set aside until needed.

2. **Choux Pastry for Gougère:** Heat water and butter in medium saucepan until boiling. Remove from burner; add flour, salt and pepper all at once. Stir with wooden spoon until mixture forms a ball. Return to burner; cook and stir for 2 minutes. Cool slightly.

3. Add eggs one at a time, beating well after each one and adding only enough of the final egg to make a mixture that is still stiff and not runny. Stir in diced cheese.

4. **To assemble:** Butter a 10-inch ovenproof skillet or shallow baking dish. Spoon gougère mixture in mounds around edge of pan to form a ring, leaving the centre open. Spoon filling into centre. Sprinkle with shredded Cheddar.

5. Bake in preheated 400° F oven for 40 minutes, or until gougère is puffed and brown and filling is bubbling.

6. Sprinkle with parsley and cut into wedges. Serve directly from pan.

Leanne's comment:

WOW! This gougère will make guests go gaga! A divine brunch entree.

Perfect Choux Pastry

Choux or cream puff pastry must be just the right texture if the puffs are to rise properly when baked. Avoid a mixture that flattens into a puddle: the puffs will not puff! Beat well after adding each egg. To ensure that the mixture is thick enough, beat in the final egg a little at a time. The mixture should be stiff and still mound well.

Variation

This sauce is also great on chicken!

Southwest Barbecue Menu

Mexican Chili Dip
(page 12)

Texas-Style Ribs and Chicken

Southwest Potato Salad
(page 91)

Corn on the Cob

Green Salad with Avocado Garnish

Cowboy Cookies
(page 101)

Ice Cream

Texas-Style Ribs   Serves 4

Be sure to hand out damp hand towels when you serve these. They really *are* finger-lickin' good!

> 2 strips pork back ribs, cut into 1- or 2-rib pieces
> 1/2 cup chopped onion
> 2 cloves garlic, minced
> 1 tablespoon butter
> 3/4 cup each, ketchup and salsa
> 2 tablespoons each, brown sugar, vinegar, molasses and water
> 2 teaspoons each, lemon juice and mustard
> 1/4 teaspoon each, cayenne and salt

1. Steam or simmer ribs 45 minutes to 1 hour, or until tender. Drain.

2. In medium saucepan sauté onion and garlic in butter until tender. Stir in ketchup, salsa, sugar, vinegar, molasses, water, lemon juice, mustard, cayenne and salt. Bring to a boil; lower heat and simmer for 15 minutes.

3. Coat ribs on all sides with sauce. Grill until well cooked on all sides, being careful not to burn. Brush with sauce during grilling.

Baked Sea Bass with Tomatoes

Serves 4

Shortly after a "working trip" to Greece to learn about olive oil, Elizabeth Baird and I spent an afternoon in her kitchen recreating some of the fabulous food we had enjoyed on the trip. This dish is my version of the sea bass entree we prepared that day.

Olive oil
1 small onion, thinly sliced
1 stalk celery, thinly sliced
2 tablespoons fresh lemon juice
1 teaspoon dried oregano
1 large clove garlic, minced
1 1/2 cups chopped ripe tomatoes, or drained canned Italian
    tomatoes, chopped
1 5- to 6-ounce piece firm-fleshed fish per person (sea bass, halibut,
    kingfish, tilapia, monkfish, etc.)
Salt and pepper
Lemon juice
Parsley, minced

Buying Fish

Make friends with your fishmonger! He will tell you what's new and what's fresh, and suggest interesting ways to cook your "catch of the day".

1. Pour enough olive oil into a skillet to cover bottom. Heat, then add onion, celery, lemon juice and oregano. Cook and stir over medium heat until vegetables are soft. Add garlic and tomatoes; bring to boil. Cook for 5 minutes.

2. Rinse fish with cold water; pat dry with paper towels. Remove bones and skin if desired. Place fish pieces in baking dish. Sprinkle with salt, pepper and lemon juice. Spoon tomato mixture over. Bake at 350° F for 25 to 30 minutes, or until fish is opaque and flakes with a fork. Sprinkle with minced fresh parsley and serve at once, with hot cooked rice or Greek Roasted Potatoes (page 88).

Paella is pronounced

"pie-eh-yaw"

(That's the
Canadian *eh*!)

Paella Alfresco

Serves 8 to 12

This is picnic food in Spain where paella is cooked in large flat pans over an open fire, adding whatever meat, shellfish and poultry is available. It's a good meal to make at the cottage when you have lots of house guests to help with the preparation. In the winter, Read sets up a sturdy grill in our fireplace so that we can share this Spanish feast with friends.

12 to 24 medium shrimp
12 clams
12 mussels
1 pound spicy smoked sausage
12 serving pieces chicken
Salt and pepper, to taste
1/3 cup olive oil, divided
2 large cloves garlic, minced
1/2 cup chopped onion
1 red pepper, thinly sliced
2 tomatoes, seeded, chopped
3 cups long-grain rice
1/4 teaspoon saffron, crushed
1 teaspoon salt
6 cups chicken stock, boiling
1/2 cup peas
2 lemons, each cut into 6 wedges

1. Shell and devein shrimp. Set aside. Scrub clams and mussels thoroughly under cold running water. Set aside. Slice sausage into 1/2-inch rounds; set aside.

2. Season chicken with salt and pepper and cook in 3 tablespoons olive oil large skillet over medium-high heat until brown on all sides. Remove from pan; set aside.

3. To make Sofrito: Remove excess fat from same large skillet. Add remaining olive oil; cook garlic, onions, red pepper and tomatoes over medium-high heat 5 minutes or until most of the moisture evaporates.

4. Preheat gas barbecue to hot, or charcoal to white-hot coals. Grill should be 3 inches above coals. Grill must be sturdy.

5. In large skillet or paella pan over medium heat, combine sofrito, rice, saffron and 1 teaspoon salt. Add boiling stock; stir to mix well. Quickly arrange chicken, sausage and seafood on top, making sure that clams and mussels have their hinges facing down. Scatter peas on top.

6. Transfer pan to barbecue and let paella cook briskly, undisturbed for 15 to 18 minutes, or until all liquid is absorbed. Do not stir during cooking.

7. When paella is done, remove from grill, cover with towel or foil and let stand for 5 minutes.

8. Serve directly from pan, garnished with lemon wedges.

Variations

Substitute rabbit for chicken. Lobster, squid, crab legs or snails may be added. Replace peas with green beans or artichokes.

Leanne's comment:

My husband couldn't stop talking about this meal at Pam's fireside. The flavour was spectacular. Cooking dinner in a huge cast-iron skillet over an open fire...another rush altogether!

Saffron

The yellow orange stigmas from a tiny purple crocus. Very expensive to buy because it's very labour intensive to harvest by hand. Used to add distinct flavour and yellow tint to many dishes including paella, risotto and bouillabaisse. Buy saffron threads rather than ground saffron for best flavour. Crush just before using. Store in an airtight container in a cool, dark place for up to 6 months.

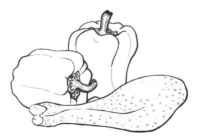

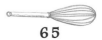

How to Make a Grill Basket

(For kebobs, burgers, fish fillets or steaks, shrimp, etc.)

Use two well-oiled cake cooling racks. Place food to be grilled on one rack. Top with second rack. Tie corners together using twist ties with metal centres. This method will keep delicate fleshed fish from falling apart during cooking, make it easier and quicker to rotate a number of items efficiently and keep small items from falling into the barbecue.

Maple Orange Glazed Salmon

Serves 4

The perfect entree for a quick meal. Tastes great, after only a few minutes of marinating. I made this recipe for two of my sisters, Cathy and Mary Pat, and each of them have made it often ever since. Mary Pat suggests that most people will not be satisfied with a 4-ounce piece of salmon, so shop accordingly.

1/2 cup orange juice concentrate
1/2 cup maple syrup
1 clove garlic, crushed
2 tablespoons dark soy sauce
4 4- to 6-ounce salmon fillets or steaks
Orange slices, to garnish
Parsley sprigs, to garnish

1. In flat glass dish large enough to hold salmon in a single layer, combine orange juice concentrate, maple syrup, garlic and soy sauce. Stir well to mix.

2. Place salmon in marinade, turning over to coat well on both sides. Marinate in refrigerator up to 4 hours, spooning marinade over occasionally during first 5 minutes of grilling. Grill salmon for 10 minutes per inch of thickness, measured at thickest part of piece. Salmon is done when it is opaque and flakes easily with a fork. Garnish with sliced oranges and parsley sprigs.

Variations:
1. Substitute boneless skinless chicken breasts for the salmon. Remove fillets from each breast piece. Flatten chicken breasts between two pieces of plastic wrap to shorten grilling time. Grill until chicken feels springy to the touch and no pink colour remains when you cut into thickest piece.
2. Pork tenderloin also works well in this recipe. Grill over hot coals for 15 to 20 minutes, turning often, until pork reaches internal temperature of 160° F on a meat thermometer. Let stand 5 minutes before slicing.

Leanne's comment:

I am a Maritimer and finicky about how fish is treated. This is a swimmingly delicious fish treat.

(photo on back cover)

Garden Vegetable Pizza

Serves 4 to 6

A quick supper dish to serve when harvest vegetables are at their best, or anytime you want a light-tasting meal.

    1 recipe pizza or bread dough
    1/4 to 1/2 cup Pesto Sauce (*see page 81*)
    Tomatoes, thinly sliced
    Vegetables, thinly sliced or chopped, your choice of
        sweet fresh or roasted bell peppers, zucchini, broccoli, carrots,
        sauteed onions or leek
    Parmesan cheese, grated
    Mozzarella, shredded
    Basil and parsley, minced fresh
    Drizzle of extra virgin or spicy olive oil
    Salt and pepper, to taste

1. If using frozen dough, defrost completely. Spread dough as thinly as possible on a lightly greased baking sheet or pizza pan. Spread pesto in an even layer on dough. Arrange tomato slices and vegetables of choice in an attractive pattern on pesto. Sprinkle with desired amount of Parmesan, mozzarella and half of the herbs (reserve some to sprinkle on cooked pizza) Drizzle pizza very sparingly with oil. Sprinkle lightly with salt and pepper.

2. Bake in preheated 425° F oven for 10 to 15 minutes, or until crust is nicely browned and vegetables are tender. Sprinkle with more herbs before serving.

Peeling Garlic

To easily remove the skin from a clove of garlic, place clove on cutting board, cover with the flat side of a large knife and hit knife blade to flatten the garlic. Remove skin; chop garlic.

Flavoured Garlic Oil

Peel and crush 1 clove garlic. Place in small glass jar with extra virgin olive oil and your choice of chopped fresh or dried herbs, freshly ground pepper and a pinch of cayenne or hot pepper flakes. Label and write date on jar, refrigerate and use within one week.

Onions

Generally speaking, when a recipe calls for an onion, use the following guide:

1 small onion =
1/3 to 1/2 cup chopped onion

1 medium onion = 3/4 to 1 cup chopped

1 large onion = 1 1/2 cups or more

North Gower is pronounced "North Gore"

North Gower Farmers' Market Potato Pancakes

Makes 18 to 20 pancakes

We offered samples of these crisp potato pancakes at our local farmers market one chilly fall day and could hardly keep up with the demand. We couldn't determine whether applesauce or sour cream was the preferred garnish. The number of servings you get from one batch depends on how hungry you are! Reheat leftovers as a side dish the next day.

3 eggs, beaten
3 tablespoons flour
2 pounds potatoes, scrubbed, coarsely grated
1 medium onion, coarsely grated
1 1/2 teaspoons salt
1 teaspoon sugar
Pepper to taste
Toppings: applesauce, sour cream or yogurt

1. Mix eggs and flour together in medium bowl. Stir in potatoes, onion, salt, sugar and pepper.

2. Into large non-stick skillet, pour enough oil to coat bottom. Heat until hot. Spoon about 3 tablespoons of potato mixture into skillet; flatten into a thin round. Cook until first side is golden. Turn over and cook other side until golden and crisp. Drain on paper towels and serve at once. Add more oil to skillet as needed. Serve at once or keep warm in a 200° F oven.

Couscous with Fruit   Serves 6

Take a container of instant couscous on your next camping trip. Mix with boiling water or stock, add vegetables and herbs, and dinner is served.

> 1/3 cup chopped dried apricots
> 1/2 cup golden raisins
> 1 cup boiling water
> 1 cup instant couscous
> 1 1/2 cups boiling water (*2nd amount*)
> 1 teaspoon minced fresh ginger
> 1 orange, peeled, diced
> 1/2 cup slivered almonds, toasted

Dressing:
> 2 tablespoons orange juice
> 1 tablespoon fresh lemon juice
> 1/4 cup olive oil
> Zest of 1 orange
> Dash of nutmeg
> 1/4 cup chopped fresh mint
> Salt and pepper to taste

1. Place apricots and raisins in medium bowl. Pour 1 cup boiling water over. Let stand 1/2 hour; drain.

2. Combine couscous, 1 1/2 cups boiling water and the minced fresh ginger in a bowl; let stand for 10 minutes, or until couscous is chewable and all water is absorbed. Fluff couscous with fork. Stir in oranges.

3. Measure dressing ingredients into jar with tight fitting lid; shake well. Taste and adjust seasonings.

4. Stir apricot mixture and dressing into couscous. Taste; season if necessary. Cover and refrigerate.

5. Stir in almonds just before serving.

Scissors Are Best

Instead of a knife, use scissors for snipping herbs such as parsley or dill; for chopping or slivering dried fruits such as apricots; and for cutting up sun-dried tomatoes.

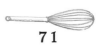

Orzo

Orzo is the Italian word for barley. Orzo is actually tiny rice-shaped pasta that cooks quickly and can be used in soups, salads and side dishes in place of rice.

Lentil and Orzo Greek Salad

Serves 4

The bright colours and various textures of the ingredients of this Mediterranean side dish will make your next barbecue a meal to remember. An added bonus: Lentils are an excellent source of vegetable protein.

Salad:

 1/2 cup lentils
 1/4 cup orzo (rice-shaped pasta)
 Water
 1/2 cup each, chopped red, yellow and green peppers
 1/2 cup chopped cucumbers
 2 small tomatoes, seeded, chopped
 2 green onions, chopped
 1 small zucchini, thinly sliced
 1 tablespoon each, chopped fresh dill and parsley (1 teaspoon dried)
 1 teaspoon chopped fresh oregano (1/2 teaspoon dried)
 1/2 cup crumbled feta cheese
 1/3 cup whole or sliced kalamata olives

Vinaigrette:

 Juice of 1/2 lemon
 1 tablespoon red wine vinegar
 1 large clove garlic, minced, or 2 to 3 cloves roasted garlic (*page 40*)
 1 teaspoon each chopped fresh oregano, parsley and basil
 1/2 teaspoon salt, or to taste
 Freshly ground pepper, to taste
 1/3 cup olive or canola oil

1. Place lentils in medium saucepan with enough water to cover by 2 inches. Add 1/2 teaspoon salt and 1/2 teaspoon oil. Bring to a boil. Cover pot, lower heat and simmer for 20 minutes or until lentils are almost tender. Stir in orzo; simmer 5 minutes, or until orzo is tender. Drain well. Refrigerate until cold. (If you prefer, lentils and orzo can be cooked separately.)

2. In large bowl, combine lentil mixture with remaining salad ingredients except feta and olives. Stir to mix.

3. Measure vinaigrette ingredients into a jar with a tight-fitting lid. If using roasted garlic, crush it with a fork and mix it with lemon juice before adding remaining ingredients so that garlic blends in well. Shake vinaigrette well; stir into salad. Taste and adjust seasonings.

4. Spoon salad into serving bowl. Garnish with feta and olives.

Lentils

There are many sizes, shapes and colours of lentils to choose from. All but the tiny red, or Egyptian, lentils still have their seed coats on, so will take longer to cook than red lentils. Because they have no outer shells, red lentils tend to break up and become a purée when cooked. All lentils are sold dried and should be stored in airtight containers. Before cooking, rinse lentils in a sieve and discard small twigs and stones that may be present. Cooked lentils can be frozen.

How to Cook Grains

Millet:

Rinse well. Cook in double volume of water. Add millet to rapidly boiling water. Simmer in covered saucepan for 15 minutes, or until tender.

Bulghur:

Pour double volume of boiling liquid over dry bulghur. Let stand for 15 to 20 minutes, or until liquid is absorbed.

Couscous:

Pour double volume boiling liquid over couscous; let stand 5 minutes, or until liquid is absorbed.

Millet and Vegetable Pilaf

Serves 4

Don't think millet is just for the birds. It's a healthy addition to the human diet as well.

    1 large carrot, scrubbed and diced
    1 medium onion, peeled and chopped
    1 large rib of celery, sliced
    1/4 cup chopped green pepper
    1/2 teaspoon dried basil or oregano
    1 tablespoon oil
    1/2 teaspoon salt, or to taste
    1 1/4 cups chicken stock or water
    1/2 cup millet
    1/2 cup shredded Cheddar or mozzarella cheese
    Pepper, to taste
    2 tablespoons minced fresh parsley

1. Sauté vegetables, basil and oil in a large pot until softened. Add salt and stock or water and stir. Bring to boil. Add millet and stir. Cover and cook on medium-low for 20 minutes or until millet is tender. Add a bit more stock during cooking if the mixture dries out.

2. Stir in cheese, pepper and parsley and more salt if needed. Serve as soon as cheese melts.

Wheat Berry Vegetable Salad

Serves 4 to 6

This tasty and colourful salad can be made with barley if desired. Add cooked beef, chicken or shellfish to make it the main attraction.

Salad:

- 1 cup dried wheat berries (soft wheat kernels)
- 1/2 cup each, chopped red and green pepper
- 1/4 cup chopped fresh parsley
- 2 tablespoons chopped green onion
- Optional: chopped tomatoes, chopped cucumber, crumbled feta, black olives, snipped fresh dill to taste

Vinaigrette:

- 1 tablespoon lemon juice
- 1 tablespoon balsamic vinegar
- 2 tablespoons olive oil
- Tabasco sauce, to taste
- 1/2 teaspoon Dijon mustard
- Salt & pepper, to taste

1. To cook wheat berries: Rinse wheat berries. Place in saucepan; cover with cold water to cover by at least 1 inch. Bring to boil; lower heat and simmer 1 1/2 hours or until wheat berries are tender but still chewy. Check often and add water as needed to keep level 1 inch above wheat berries. When cooked, drain well. In large bowl, mix together all salad ingredients.

2. In small bowl, whisk together vinaigrette ingredients. Pour over salad; mix well. Refrigerate until cold.

3. Just before serving, taste and adjust seasonings. Spoon into serving bowl.

Wheat Berries

Wheat berries are whole, unprocessed kernels of soft or hard wheat and can be purchased in bulk-food stores. They take a long time to cook, but freeze well once cooked. Cook double the amount you need and freeze half to ensure that you will have them on hand when you need them for recipes such as this.

(photo on back cover, with salmon)

How to Cook Grains

Barley:

Cook in large saucepan with four times more water or stock than barley. Bring to boil, then lower heat and simmer until tender, about 45 minutes. Check often and add more liquid as needed. Drain off excess liquid when barley is cooked.

Quinoa:

Spread quinoa on a shallow dish; remove any pieces of grit. Rinse quinoa well. Cook in double volume of water. Bring to boil. Simmer 15 minutes or until tender and nearly transparent. Drain off any liquid that remains.

Asparagus Quick Tips:

Make your favourite dill pickle recipe, substituting asparagus spears. Add 1 hot pepper if desired. Process filled 1-pint jars in boiling water bath for 15 minutes.

Brush spears with oil and vinegar dressing, then grill on the barbecue.

Wrap lightly steamed or pickled asparagus spears in thinly sliced prosciutto. Drizzle with olive oil and lemon juice or wine vinegar.

Pasta Primavera with Asparagus   Serves 4 to 6

I start checking my asparagus patch for sprouts almost as soon as the snow disappears! Who can resist the flavour asparagus gives to dishes such as this light and healthy pasta.

1 medium onion, chopped
2 cloves garlic, minced
1 tablespoon olive oil or butter
1 cup sliced mushrooms
1 cup chopped red bell pepper
1 pound asparagus spears, in 1 1/2-inch diagonal slices
1 tablespoon dried basil (*3 tablespoons fresh*)
1/2 teaspoon each, salt and pepper
3 tablespoons flour
2 cups milk
350 g package fusilli or rotini pasta, cooked and drained
2/3 cup grated Parmesan
Minced fresh parsley and basil to taste

1. In large non-stick skillet, sauté onion and garlic in oil or butter over medium-high heat until onion softens. Stir in remaining vegetables; cook and stir for 5 to 7 minutes, or until tender.

2. Stir in basil, salt, pepper and flour; slowly add milk. Cook and stir 5 minutes, or until sauce thickens. Stir in hot pasta; mix well. Add Parmesan, more pepper if desired and minced parsley and basil to taste. Toss and serve immediately.

Leanne's comment:

This pasta is a visual feast and tastes even better.

Pasta with Sun-Dried Tomato Sauce

Serves 4 to 6

A rich and creamy pasta sauce enhanced with the flavour of sun-dried tomatoes. So quick and easy that you can make it in the time it takes to cook the pasta.

2 tablespoons butter
2 cloves garlic, minced
2 tablespoons flour
1 1/2 cups milk
2 tablespoons fresh basil (*2 teaspoons dried*)
15 to 20 sun-dried tomatoes
450 g fresh pasta (*350 g dried*)
1/3 cup minced parsley
Salt and pepper
Parmesan cheese, grated

1. Simmer garlic in butter in medium saucepan on stove or in microwave (High for 1 1/2 minutes) until garlic is soft. Stir in flour; whisk in milk. Cook and stir over medium heat until slightly thickened.

2. Cut tomatoes into strips. Add to sauce, along with basil. Let stand for 5 minutes, or until tomatoes soften.

3. Cook pasta and drain. Toss with sauce. Add parsley, salt and pepper to taste. Sprinkle each serving with Parmesan and serve immediately.

Leanne's comment:

Pasta ... yum, yum, yum! Whether you are energetic and Pam convinces you to put the 'elbow' grease into homemade pasta or you open a package...you can't go wrong with these recipes. Pam and I often joke we've never met a carbohydrate we didn't like. These pasta dishes will give you that same pleasure.

Sun-Dried Tomatoes

Available in the produce department of most supermarkets. Drying strengthens the tomato flavour and results in a product that is chewy, quite sweet and should be leathery in texture rather than dry and hard. Sun-dried tomatoes are usually softened before using by soaking in warm water for 5 to 10 minutes, then patting dry. I sometimes chop them finely with scissors (without soaking) and add to tomato-based pasta sauces and soups to intensify the tomato flavour.

Parmesan: Choose the Best!

Avoid the containers of pre-grated cheese stored at room temperature on store shelves. This has the poorest flavour. Buy Parmesan by the piece and grate it as needed for most intense flavour. Wrapped well, it will keep in the refrigerator for several weeks.

Parmigiano Reggiano—the very best and, of course, most expensive.

Grana Padano— still very good quality.

Pasta with Fresh Tomatoes and Basil

Serves 4 to 6

There is no better summer pasta dish than this to serve with grilled meat, poultry or fish. Grow tomatoes and basil side by side in your garden—they are the perfect complement to each other.

1/4 cup extra virgin olive oil
3 large ripe tomatoes, chopped
2 cloves garlic, crushed or minced
1/2 cup slivered fresh basil leaves
450 g fresh (*or 350 g dried*) fettucine, cooked and drained
Salt and freshly ground pepper to taste
Parmesan cheese, grated

1. In bottom of large serving dish, stir together oil, tomatoes, garlic and basil. Let stand at room temperature for a few minutes to blend flavours.

2. Add hot cooked pasta; toss until well mixed. Season to taste with salt, pepper and Parmesan. Serve at once.

Pasta with Toasted Walnuts

Serves 4

The crunchy butter-browned walnuts add a wonderful flavour and texture to this simple side dish.

2 tablespoons butter
1/2 cup chopped walnuts
Dash salt and paprika
1/2 of a 375 g package of egg noodles, cooked and drained
2 teaspoons minced fresh parsley

1. In small saucepan, melt butter until bubbly; stir in walnuts. Cook and stir over medium-low heat until walnuts are light brown. Stir in salt and paprika. Set aside.

2. At serving time, toss warm walnut mixture with freshly cooked, hot pasta and minced parsley. Serve at once.

Make Ahead

Prepare the walnut mixture early in the day and refrigerate in a small microwave-safe dish. At serving time, warm the mixture briefly in the microwave before tossing with freshly cooked pasta.

Freezer Spaghetti Sauce

Makes 16 cups

Make this in the fall when tomatoes are plentiful and tasty. Use it to sauce your favourite pasta, or use it as a base for a hearty vegetable soup.

Fill large pot with water; bring to boil. Cut stem end out of tomatoes. Place tomatoes in boiling water for 20 to 30 seconds or until skin loosens. When cool enough to handle, slip off skin.

2 cups chopped onion
2 large cloves garlic, minced
1/3 cup olive oil
12 cups peeled, chopped tomatoes
2 cups dry red wine (*or water*)
1 1/2 cups tomato paste
2 beef cubes, crumbled
1/4 cup fresh basil leaves, chopped (*4 teaspoons dried*), or to taste
2 bay leaves
2 teaspoons salt
Pepper, to taste

1. Sauté onion, garlic and oil in large saucepan until onion is soft. Add remaining ingredients. Bring to boil over medium heat. Lower heat to low; simmer gently for 1 to 1 1/2 hours, or until sauce is thickened. Stir occasionally.

2. Remove bay leaves and cool slightly. Spoon mixture into serving-sized containers; seal, label and freeze.

3. To serve as a pasta sauce for 4 people, combine 2 to 4 cups of sauce with 1 small tin of tomato paste. If desired, add 3/4 to 1 pound of cooked meat, fish or poultry. Add chopped, roasted tomatoes (*page 92*) or slivered sun-dried tomatoes, if available, especially if sauce is served without added meat, fish or poultry.

Pesto Sauce: Two Versions

Summer Pesto

Makes approximately 1 1/2 cups

Make this pesto when fresh basil is plentiful and affordable. Be sure to plant lots of basil in your garden; pesto freezes well.

> 2 cups (*packed*) fresh basil leaves
> 2 cloves garlic
> 3 tablespoons pine nuts or walnuts, toasted
> 1/4 to 1/2 cup olive oil
> 3/4 cup grated Parmesan cheese
> Salt and pepper, to taste

1. In blender or food processor, blend together basil, garlic, pine nuts, and enough oil to make mixture smooth.

2. Transfer to bowl; stir in Parmesan. Add salt and pepper to taste. If too thick, add 1 to 2 teaspoons hot water or a bit more oil. Store in refrigerator for up to one week, or in freezer.

All~Seasons Pesto Sauce

Makes 1 cup

Make this when the only fresh basil you can find comes in tiny bunches and costs a fortune.

> 1 1/2 tablespoons pine nuts or walnuts, toasted
> 1 cup (*packed*) spinach leaves (*no stems*)
> 1/4 cup chopped fresh parsley
> 1 clove garlic
> 1 teaspoon dried basil leaves
> 1/4 teaspoon salt
> 1/3 cup olive oil
> 1/3 cup grated Parmesan cheese

1. Place nuts, spinach, parsley, garlic, basil, salt and oil in blender or food processor; process until smooth.

2. Transfer to bowl. Stir in Parmesan. Taste and add salt and pepper as needed. Will keep refrigerated for one week. Freezes well.

Money-Saving Tip

Replace up to half of the wild rice with white rice in this and other similar wild rice recipes. Because they take different times to cook, cook each rice separately and then mix together.

Leannes's Wild Rice with Almonds, Raisins and Port

Serves 6

A festive side dish to enhance your holiday or special occasion meals.

1/2 cup raisins
1/4 cup port
5 cups chicken stock
1 1/2 cups wild rice, rinsed
1/2 cup slivered almonds
1 tablespoon butter
Salt and pepper to taste

1. Place raisins and port in small bowl; stir. Let stand for 1 hour.

2. Measure water or stock into a large saucepan; if using water, add salt. Bring to boil over high heat. Stir in wild rice; lower heat to medium-low; boil gently for 45 minutes, or until rice is tender. Drain off remaining liquid through a sieve.

3. While rice cooks, toast almonds in butter in small skillet over medium heat, stirring frequently until lightly browned. Transfer mixture to bowl; set aside.

4. To serve, mix together rice, almonds and raisin mixture including port. Season lightly with salt and pepper. Spoon into serving bowl. Serve hot. (Can be prepared ahead and reheated.)

Cooking White Rice in the Microwave

When you cook rice in the microwave, you never have to worry about it burning and sticking to the bottom of the pot.

For 3 cups of cooked rice: bring 2 cups water and 1 teaspoon salt to boil in a 6-cup microwave-safe casserole or measuring cup. Stir in 1 cup long grain rice. Cover and microwave on Medium-low for 15 minutes, or until all liquid is absorbed. Fluff with a fork.

Broccoli and Carrot Casserole   Serves 8 to 10

Because this can be assembled a day ahead, it is a perfect addition to any buffet or holiday dinner menus.

> 4 cups bite-sized broccoli florets, cooked to tender-crisp, drained
> 4 cups sliced carrots, cooked to tender-crisp, drained
> 1/4 cup butter
> 1 cup chopped onion
> 1 teaspoon salt, or to taste
> 1/2 teaspoon pepper
> 1/4 cup flour
> 2 cups light sour cream (or *plain low-fat yogurt*)
> 1/3 cup dry breadcrumbs
> 1/3 cup grated Cheddar cheese
> Paprika

1. Sauté onion in butter in large saucepan over medium heat until soft but not brown. Stir in salt, pepper and flour. Stir in sour cream or yogurt; mix well. Cook and stir until mixture is hot.

2. Add cooked broccoli and carrots to sour cream mixture. Transfer to buttered casserole dish.

3. Sprinkle breadcrumbs and cheese over casserole if you plan to bake in the oven. For microwave, refrigerate casserole and toppings separately, as casserole must be stirred during microwave cooking. Cover and refrigerate until baking time, overnight if necessary. Remove from refrigerator 30 minutes before baking.

4. **To heat in the microwave**: Uncover the casserole and microwave on High for 7 to 9 minutes, or until heated through. Stir several times during heating. Sprinkle crumbs and cheese over before serving. Let stand until cheese melts, or broil to melt cheese. If desired, sprinkle with paprika before serving.

   To heat in the oven: Bake at 400° F for 20 to 30 minutes, or until heated through.

Time Saver

Make breadcrumbs from leftover bread and rolls. Process in food processor to desired texture. If fresh, store in freezer. If dried, store in an airtight container.

Leanne's comment:
> Pam tries to make your life easier while giving delicious menu options. This is one of her make-ahead suggestions for Thanksgiving or Christmas. It is colourful and yummy.

83

Green Beans with Mustard Cream Sauce

Serves 6

This creamy sauce is the perfect topping for broccoli, asparagus or green beans.

1 pound fresh green beans, trimmed
1/4 cup light sour cream
1 to 2 teaspoons grainy mustard, or to taste

1. Microwave, boil or steam beans until just tender. Arrange on warm platter.

2. Combine sour cream and mustard in small saucepan or microwave-safe bowl. Heat on stove or in microwave until hot but not boiling.

3. Just before serving, drizzle sauce over beans. Serve at once.

Leanne's comment:

If you are overwhelmed by a bountiful bean harvest, this gives you a new twist on how to serve them.

Grilled Ratatouille

Serves 4

A fabulous side dish, or the main course when served with crusty bread and old Cheddar.

>   1 thick slice of Spanish onion
>   2 small zucchini, halved lengthwise
>   1 large red or green pepper, quartered
>   8 Roma tomatoes, halved lengthwise
>   1 small eggplant, cut in thick slices
>   2 cloves garlic, minced
>   1 tablespoon minced fresh basil
>   5 tablespoons olive oil
>   2 tablespoons red or white wine vinegar
>   Salt and pepper, to taste

1. Prepare vegetables as indicated. In small bowl mix together garlic, basil and olive oil. Season lightly with salt and pepper. Brush on vegetable pieces.

2. Grill vegetables over hot coals, turning often. Remove each type of vegetable from grill as soon as it is tender. Remove skin from tomatoes, pepper and eggplant.

3. Chop vegetables, then place in large bowl with remaining garlic mixture, red wine vinegar, and chopped fresh basil, and salt and pepper to taste. Chill until cold to blend flavours. Taste and adjust seasonings.

4. Serve at room temperature with crusty bread, as a side vegetable or as a topping for pizza or bruschetta.

Grilled Vegetables with Herbs and Chèvre

Serves 6

Parsley Pointer

Curly parsley can be very sandy, so wash well and dry in salad spinner until as dry as possible. The drier it is, the longer it will keep.

Wrap clean parsley loosely in paper towels and store in a plastic bag in the refrigerator.

Time Saver

Cook vegetables in grill basket for easy grilling. See How to Make a Grill Basket, page 66.

A terrific way to enjoy summer vegetables. Choose the vegetables that are freshest and best.

    1/2 cup olive oil, or as needed
    2 cloves garlic, crushed
    2 to 3 tablespoons minced fresh herbs: your choice of basil, thyme,
        oregano, dill, parsley, or chives
    Salt and pepper, to taste
    Fresh herbs, chopped
    Chèvre (*soft goat cheese*), crumbled
    Vegetables to grill (*choose your favourites*):
        3 portobello mushrooms, stems removed
        3 leeks, halved lengthwise, washed well
        2 red or yellow bell peppers, quartered
        18 asparagus stalks, trimmed
        4 to 6 eggplant slices
        3 small zucchini halved lengthwise
        6 parboiled potato halves
        4 parboiled carrots, halved lengthwise

1. Combine oil, garlic, herbs and seasonings in small bowl. Let stand for 30 minutes.

2. Prepare vegetables as indicated. Brush with herbed oil mixture. Grill to desired degree of doneness, turning often and brushing with oil during grilling.

3. Transfer vegetables to serving platter. Drizzle any remaining oil mixture over. Keep warm in 200° F oven until serving time. Just before serving, top with crumbled chèvre and chopped fresh herbs. Toss gently if desired. Serve hot.

Southwest Potato Salad

Serves 6

Even if you have a favourite potato salad, try this one. Its zippy taste is sure to please. The secret of great potato salad? Toss the potatoes while they are still warm with vinegar or lemon juice.

6 medium potatoes
1/4 cup cider vinegar
1/2 cup chopped green onion
2/3 cup light mayonnaise
1/3 cup light sour cream
3 tablespoons snipped fresh dill
1 teaspoon salt
1/2 teaspoon pepper
1 teaspoon grainy Dijon mustard
2 hard-cooked eggs, peeled and chopped (*optional*)

1. Cook potatoes in gently boiling salted water until just tender. Drain. Peel and chop into bite-sized pieces.

2. Place potatoes in large bowl. Add cider vinegar and onions; toss gently. Set aside.

3. In separate bowl, combine mayonnaise, sour cream, dill, salt, pepper and grainy Dijon. Pour over potatoes; toss gently until potatoes are well coated with mayonnaise mixture. Gently mix in eggs.

4. Spoon into serving bowl. Garnish with dill. Serve at once or cover and refrigerate. Serve at room temperature.

Potato Cooking Tip

Rapid boiling makes potatoes break up during cooking. It is better to simmer gently just until potatoes are tender. This is especially important when you are planning to chop potatoes for recipes like potato salad.

Safe Picnic Food

- Chill cooked foods thoroughly before packing into a cooler.

- Place the most perishable foods in the bottom of the cooler with the ice packs on top.

- To avoid opening the food cooler and exposing the contents to the heat, pack drinks and snack foods in a separate cooler for quick and frequent access.

Leanne's comment:

This is the only potato salad for me. It has a zing that is often missing in others.

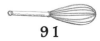

Quick Takes for Harvest Vegetables

Too Much Zucchini? Grate and freeze extra in 1-cup quantities to defrost in the microwave. Use in muffins, brownies, sauces and soups.

Quickest Way to Cook Spaghetti Squash: Wash and dry squash and pierce skin several times with a sharp knife. Place on a paper towel (if squash is wax-coated) on a microwave-safe plate and microwave on High for 5 to 7 minutes, per pound, or until squash is tender when pierced with a fork or sharp knife. Rotate squash halfway through cooking time. Let stand 5 minutes before cutting. Cut squash in half lengthwise and scoop out seeds. Use a fork to pull out and separate squash strands. Use as a substitute for pasta, topped with your favourite Italian tomato sauce or Ratatouille, and freshly grated Parmesan cheese.

Quickest Way to Cook Pumpkin, Rutabaga or Squash: Same as for Spaghetti Squash, above. Cool each vegetable 5 minutes before using in desired recipe.

Freezing and Peeling Tomatoes: To peel tomatoes easily, cut off the stem ends and freeze tomatoes in plastic bags. When ready to use, hold the frozen tomatoes under cool running water and the skins will slip right off.

Drying Herbs in the Microwave: Place 1/2 cup clean, dry, fresh herb leaves on a paper towel on a paper plate. Cover with another paper towel. Microwave on High 2 to 3 minutes, or until just crisp. Check often during cooking and do not overcook. Monitor closely throughout cooking time. Do not use the same plate and towels for 2 successive batches; they may ignite if overheated. For best results, do not try to dry more than 1/2 cup at a time.

Roasted Tomatoes: Wash 3 pounds plum or Roma tomatoes; cut in half lengthwise. Arrange tomato halves cut side up on a baking sheet with raised edges. In small bowl, mix together 2 crushed cloves of garlic and about 1/4 cup olive oil. Let stand for 15 minutes. Drizzle oil over tomatoes to coat. Sprinkle lightly with salt and pepper. Roast in 375° F oven for 1 1/2 hours, or until moisture in tomatoes is reduced by half. Cool mixture; freeze in single layer on baking sheet. When frozen, pack in small containers or plastic bags, label and freeze.

Artichoke Heart Salad

Serves 10 to 12

A great party salad to make ahead. Refrigerate washed torn salad greens in a plastic bag to be ready for the salad bowl at serving time. Prepare vinaigrette, add artichokes, peppers and anchovies, and chill until dinner is served.

Vinaigrette:
>   1/2 cup olive oil
>   1/3 cup wine vinegar (*red or white*)
>   2 tablespoons water
>   1 small onion, chopped
>   1 tablespoon sugar
>   1 large clove garlic, crushed
>   1/2 teaspoon salt
>   1/4 teaspoon celery seed
>   Pepper, to taste

Salad:
>   1 tin artichoke hearts, drained, chopped
>   1 roasted red pepper, slivered (freshly roasted or bottled)
>   1 2-ounce tin anchovies, rinsed, diced

>   Large bowl mixed greens (lettuce, spinach, radicchio, etc.)

1. In medium saucepan, heat vinaigrette ingredients to boiling. Stir in artichoke hearts; simmer gently for 5 minutes. Cool; stir in peppers and anchovies. Refrigerate until serving time.

2. To serve: Drain off vinaigrette and reserve. Toss artichoke mixture with salad greens. Add enough of the reserved vinaigrette to moisten.

Leanne's comment:

This is a salad I've served several times and the reviews are always excellent. Artichokes and anchovies...a flavour blend that tastes like more.

Potluck

Carry greens and artichoke vinaigrette to party in two separate containers. Add solids from artichoke mixture to greens; toss. Add enough vinaigrette to coat greens. Serve.

Potluck Tip

Always bring with you everything you need to serve your potluck contribution. The hostess may not have the utensils or serving dishes you require, or may be too busy to find them for you.

Avocadoes

A ripe avocado, though still firm, will yield to the touch when gently squeezed. Avocadoes should be ripened at room temperature, then refrigerated until needed. Sprinkle sliced avocado with lime or lemon juice to prevent discolouring. To prevent discolouring, peel and slice avocado as close to serving time as possible. Though high in unsaturated fat, avocadoes are also high in Vitamin C, thaimine and riboflavin. An 8-ounce avocado contains about 275 calories.

Avocado and Clementine Salad   Serves 8

I like to serve this attractive salad with Tourtière on Christmas Eve. Use navel or blood orange segments to replace the clementines if you wish.

> 4 clementine oranges, peeled, in segments
> 2 avocadoes, peeled and sliced at the last minute
> 2 heads Boston lettuce, washed, leaves separated

Vinaigrette:
Shake together in jar with a tight fitting lid:
> 2 tablespoons white wine vinegar
> 2 teaspoons sugar
> 1/2 teaspoon Dijon mustard
> 1/4 cup olive or vegetable oil
> 1 teaspoon poppy seeds
> 1/4 teaspoon salt

1. Arrange one or two lettuce leaves on each individual serving plate.

2. Just before serving, peel and slice avocadoes. Toss orange segments and avocado slices gently with vinaigrette. Arrange attractively on lettuce leaves. Serve at once.

Enjoy—Occasionally!
One of my favourite indulgences is an avocado and bacon sandwich on whole wheat toast with lots of low-fat mayonnaise! Not to be eaten every day!

Leanne's comment:
This salad was one Pam presented as popular 'retro' food. Well, it's so delicious it's timeless.

Black Bean and Corn Salad

Serves 6 to 8

Such a colourful and delicious salad to make in minutes. Easy to take along to a potluck barbecue.

    1 15-ounce tin black beans, drained and rinsed
    1 11-ounce tin kernel corn, drained
    1/2 cup each coarsely chopped green and red bell pepper
    1/2 cup slivered red onion
    1/4 cup chopped jalapeno peppers, or to taste
    1/4 cup minced fresh parsley or cilantro

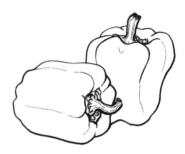

Vinaigrette:
    1/4 cup oil
    2 tablespoons red wine vinegar
    1/2 teaspoon salt
    1/4 teaspoon ground cumin
    1/4 teaspoon pepper

1. Combine salad vegetables in large bowl; toss to mix. Set aside.

2. Combine vinaigrette ingredients; shake well. Mix well with vegetables. Cover; refrigerate 1 hour to blend flavours.

 Leanne's comment: *Serve with Southwest Potato Salad, page 91. This is a cheerful combination…the perfect side to any picnic or BBQ.*

Make Ahead

If making ahead, use less of the hot chili sauce, as the heat of the chilies intensifies over time. Add more chili sauce or sambal to taste at serving time if needed.

Cucumber Salad

Serves 6

One of my favourite ways to use cucumbers. Serve as a salad or tuck the slices into your favourite sandwich.

    1 cup white vinegar
    1/4 cup water
    3 green onions, chopped
    1/4 cup sugar
    1/4 teaspoon *Sambal Oelek*, Chinese chili sauce or red pepper
        flakes to taste (*see page 44*)
    1 English cucumber, thinly sliced

1. Combine all ingredients except cucumbers in large bowl. Let stand 20 minutes.

2. Add cucumbers; stir well. Refrigerate up to two days.

Garden Tomatoes with Fresh Basil, Balsamic Vinegar and Olive Oil

I dream all year long of this mouth-watering, late August treat, made with freshly picked, sun-warmed tomatoes straight from my garden and onto my plate!

> Garden fresh tomatoes, thickly sliced
> Balsamic vinegar
> Extra virgin olive oil
> Fresh basil leaves, chopped
> Salt and pepper, to taste

1. Arrange tomato slices attractively on serving platter.

2. Drizzle lightly with small amount of balsamic vinegar and olive oil. Sprinkle with chopped basil and salt and pepper to taste. Serve at room temperature. Garnish with basil leaves and blossoms.

Tomato Tips

Store and ripen tomatoes at room temperature, never in the refrigerator.

Keep tomatoes out of direct sunlight; overheating will bake rather than ripen them.

Greek Salad

This is Greek Salad as I saw it being made in Greece. Sometimes the vegetables were assembled on a bed of slivered cabbage. Be sure to use good Greek feta cheese, extra virgin olive oil and Kalamata olives for the authentic Greek flavour.

> Fresh ripe tomatoes wedges
> Cucumber, chopped or sliced
> Green pepper, in bitesize chunks
> Red onion, thinly sliced (optional)
> Kalamata olives
> Greek feta cheese, sliced or crumbled
> Dried oregano
> Extra virgin olive oil
> Red wine vinegar

1. On individual serving plates or shallow bowls, arrange tomatoes, cucumber and green pepper pieces. Top with a few thin rings of red onion, Kalamata olives to taste and a generous slice of good Greek feta cheese (or crumble feta over if desired).

2. Sprinkle lightly with oregano. Drizzle salad with extra virgin olive oil and red wine vinegar to taste. Serve at once.

5. Bake in preheated 350° F oven for 25 to 30 minutes, or until lightly browned and firm to the touch. Let cool on baking sheet for 10 minutes.

6. Reduce oven temperature to 300° F. With serrated knife, cut logs diagonally into 1/2-inch slices; arrange slices cut side down or standing up on baking sheet. Bake 10 to 15 minutes, or until golden. Remove to wire rack; let cool completely.

Parchment Paper

Parchment paper can be purchased in rolls or sheets in supermarkets and kitchen specialty shops. It is grease and moisture resistant— like waxed paper without the wax. Besides using parchment to line baking sheets and pans for baking, use it to wrap chicken and fish to steam-roast in the oven or microwave. It can be wiped clean with a damp cloth and, unless badly stained, can be reused many times before discarding.

Edible Flowers

Flower garnishes are the quickest and easiest way to make any food look beautiful. Choose clean flowers that have not been sprayed with chemicals. Avoid commercially grown flowers unless you know they are safe to eat. *Choose from the following*: pansies, Johnny-jump-ups, rose petals, wild violets, calendulas, nasturtiums, all herb blossoms, bachelor buttons, carnations, forget-me-nots, impatiens, honeysuckle, lilac, petunias, portulaca, snapdragons, chrysanthemums, chive blossoms, day lilies, dandelions, daisies, hibiscus, scented geraniums, hollyhocks, marigolds and violas. **If you aren't sure if a flower is safe to eat, avoid it.**

Fresh Fruit Tarte

Serves 6 to 8

The no-roll pastry used for this tarte has the sweet crispness of a shortbread cookie. It's just what you need when you want to make a pie in a hurry.

Pastry:
>   1 1/2 cups flour
>   1/4 cup icing sugar
>   2/3 cup cold butter

Filling and Glaze:
>   3 to 4 cups prepared fresh fruit: berries, sliced bananas or kiwi, melon balls, thinly sliced orange (rind removed), peach slices, or any combination of fruit
>   1/4 cup fruit jelly
>   1 tablespoon fruit liqueur

Topping:
>   Sweetened whipped cream, vanilla ice cream or vanilla yogurt
>   Mint or sweet cicely sprigs and edible flowers

1. **Pastry:** Mix until crumbly flour, icing sugar and butter, either in a bowl using a pastry cutter or in a food processor using off-on pulse motion. Pour into a 9-inch flan pan or pie plate. Spread evenly over bottom and up sides. Place a piece of plastic wrap over the flan pan and use your hands to press the pastry evenly and firmly on the bottom and sides of the pan to form a pie shell.

2. Place waxed paper in flan pan to cover the pastry; fill with dried beans or pie weights. Bake in preheated 425° F oven for 8 minutes. Remove beans and paper and bake for 4 to 6 minutes more, or until pastry is golden. Cool completely.

3. Melt jelly and liqueur together. Brush a thin layer onto bottom of pastry shell. Let dry completely. Set remaining jelly aside until serving time.

4. **Filling:** Arrange fruit attractively in pastry shell as close to serving time as possible. Brush fruit and edges of pastry with remaining melted jelly. Add topping of choice. Garnish with mint or sweet cicely and edible flowers.

Maple Pecan Tarts

Makes 12 tarts

If you're pressed for time, use purchased tart shells rather than homemade pastry. These tarts taste great either way.

    24 to 36 pecan halves
    1/2 cup maple syrup
    1 egg
    1/4 cup sugar
    12 unbaked tart shells

1. Place 2 or 3 pecan halves in each tart shell. Preheat oven to 425° F.

2. Combine syrup, egg and sugar in small bowl. Stir to dissolve sugar. Pour over pecans.

3. Bake for 12 to 15 minutes, or until pastry is brown and filling is bubbly.

Attractive Garnish with Leftover Pastry

If you have leftover pastry scraps, roll thinly and use small cookie cutters to make tiny toppers for your tarts. Set in place on the filling and sprinkle lightly with granulated, brown or maple sugar before baking.

For Maple Pecan Tarts, a tiny maple leaf cutter would be most appropriate.

Baking Made Easier

To avoid spilling the filling while placing the pie in the oven, pour half of mixture into pie shell, transfer pie to preheated oven, then pour in remaining filling.

Quick Pie Baking with Microwave Help

Assemble one- or two-crust pie in a pie plate that is both microwave-safe and oven-proof. Glass works well. Preheat regular oven to 425° F. Microwave pie on High for 8 to 10 minutes, or until filling bubbles. Transfer to preheated oven; bake for 15 minutes, or until topping is golden.

Pumpkin Pie

Makes 1 deep 9-inch pie

This recipe has been very slightly modified from the original that I have been making for over 30 years from *The Laura Secord Cookbook*. I would love to see that cookbook reprinted—many pages in my copy are food-splattered, sticky and very well used.

> 2 eggs
> 1 cup evaporated milk (*skim or 2%*) or light cream
> 1 1/2 cups pumpkin purée
> 1 1/3 cups packed brown sugar
> 1 teaspoon cinnamon
> 1/2 teaspoon each, salt, ground ginger and nutmeg
> 1/4 teaspoon ground cloves
> 1 unbaked 9-inch deep pie shell (*see No-Fail Pastry recipe, page 57*)

1. In large bowl, whisk together all ingredients except pie shell. Pour mixture into pie shell.

2. Bake in preheated 450° F oven for 10 minutes. Lower oven temperature to 350° F. Bake for 45 to 50 minutes more, or until filling is set. (Insert a sharp knife blade into centre of pie; if it comes out clean, pie is cooked.)

Pumpkin Pointers

• Choose small sugar pumpkins for baking or cooking; the flesh is less watery and the flavour is better. Wash and dry skin of pumpkin. Remove stem.
• To cook in microwave: With a sharp knife blade, cut several slashes in skin of pumpkin. Weigh pumpkin. Microwave on High for 6 to 7 minutes per pound, or until sharp knife blade penetrates easily into the pumpkin. When cool enough to handle, cut pumpkin in half, scoop out seeds, remove skin and purée or mash pulp. Freeze in quantities needed for your favourite recipes.
• Dice and freeze raw pumpkin for soups and stews.
• Add grated raw pumpkin to meatloaf mixture, meatballs or stuffing for turkey or chicken.
• Roasted pumpkin seeds: Clean seeds, removing pulp and fibres. Do not wash. Sprinkle lightly with canola oil and salt. Spread on baking sheet. Roast at 250° F for 30 to 45 minutes, or until crisp and brown. Store in an airtight container.

Apple Cake

Makes 1 9-inch cake

The number of requests for recipes from our "A is for Apple" show in 1997 was one of the highest ever. The recipe for this moist, wonderful cake came from my dear friend Patti Miller of Bozeman, Montana. I've made it many times over many years.

> 4 apples, peeled, chopped
> 1 egg plus 2 egg whites
> 1/4 cup vegetable oil
> 3/4 cup sugar
> 1 teaspoon vanilla
> 1 cup all-purpose flour
> 1 teaspoon cinnamon
> 1 rounded teaspoon baking soda
> 1/4 teaspoon salt
> 2/3 cup chopped nuts (optional)

1. Measure all ingredients into large bowl in order given. Stir until well mixed, but do not beat. Spoon batter into a lightly greased 9-inch square or round baking pan. Bake in preheated 350° F oven for 35 minutes, or until toothpick inserted into cake comes out clean. Serve warm, plain or with vanilla ice cream or sweetened whipped cream.

Baking Tip

To make it easier to remove squares and cakes from the baking pan, line the pan with greased foil before adding batter. Once baked, the contents can be easily lifted out of the pan intact.

Hazelnut Torte

Serves 6 to 8

There cannot possibly be an easier cake to make than this one from my friend Carol Jukes in Vancouver. Process the cake ingredients in a food processor or blender in seconds, mix up the mocha filling while the cake layers bake, then frost it quickly with unsweetened whipped cream before serving. I try to always have an unfrosted hazelnut torte in the freezer, ready to coat with whipped cream for a quick but elegant dessert.

Cake:

> 4 eggs
> 2 tablespoons flour
> 3/4 cup sugar
> 2 1/2 teaspoons baking powder
> 1 cup hazelnuts or filberts

Filling:

> 2 tablespoons soft butter
> 1 to 1 1/2 cups icing sugar
> 1 tablespoon strong coffee
> 1 teaspoon cocoa
> 1/4 teaspoon vanilla

Topping:

> 1 cup whipping cream, whipped
> 8 to 10 whole hazelnuts
> Cocoa

1. Butter and flour two round 9-inch cake pans. Preheat oven 350° F.

2. In blender or food processor blend all cake ingredients until mixture is smooth and nuts are very finely chopped. Pour batter into prepared pans.

3. Bake for 20 minutes, or until cakes test done with a toothpick. Remove from pans after 10 minutes. Cool completely on racks.

4. For filling: cream together butter and 1 cup icing sugar. Add remaining ingredients; beat until smooth. Add more sugar if too thin to spread.

5. Spread filling on one cake. Top with second cake (can be wrapped and frozen at this point). Place cake on serving plate; cover top and sides completely with whipped cream. Smooth top. Arrange hazelnuts on top, then dust hazelnuts lightly with sieved cocoa. Serve at once or refrigerate several hours or overnight.

(*photo on back cover*)

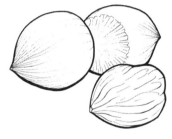

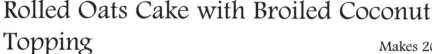

Rolled Oats Cake with Broiled Coconut Topping

Makes 20 pieces

You can always count on *Canadian Living* magazine's food director Elizabeth Baird for recipes that are easy to make and absolutely delicious. This cake, from *Elizabeth Baird's Favourites,* has become a Collacott favourite as well. It is moist, sweet comfort food at its best.

Cake:

        1 cup rolled or quick oats
        1 1/2 cups boiling water
        1/2 cup soft butter
        1 3/4 cups firmly packed brown sugar
        2 eggs
        1 teaspoon vanilla
        1 1/2 cups all-purpose flour
        1 teaspoon baking soda
        1/2 teaspoon each, salt, cinnamon and nutmeg

Topping:

        1/4 cup soft butter
        1/2 cup firmly packed brown sugar
        3 tablespoons light cream or milk
        3/4 cup shredded unsweetened coconut

1. In small bowl, combine oats and boiling water; set aside for 20 minutes.

2. In large bowl, cream together butter with brown sugar. Stir in eggs; beat well. Stir in vanilla and the oat mixture.

3. In medium bowl, stir together flour, baking soda, salt, nutmeg and cinnamon. Add to oats mixture; stir to mix well. Spoon batter into greased 9-inch square cake pan. Bake in preheated 350° F oven for 55 minutes, or until cake springs back when lightly touched.

4. To prepare topping: cream together butter and brown sugar. Mix in cream or milk and coconut. Spread this mixture evenly and gently over hot cake. Broil 4 inches from heat for 2 to 3 minutes, or until slightly browned and bubbly. Cool. Store in pan. Freezes well.

Zucchini Chocolate Cake   Makes one 8-inch cake

This is a lovely, moist chocolate cake, perfect for packed lunches.

    1/4 cup margarine or butter, softened
    3/4 cup sugar
    3 tablespoons oil
    1 egg
    1/2 teaspoon vanilla
    3 tablespoons sour milk or buttermilk
    2 1/2 tablespoons cocoa
    1/4 teaspoon baking powder
    1/2 teaspoon baking soda
    1/4 teaspoon cinnamon
    1 1/4 cups all-purpose flour
    1 cup finely grated zucchini
    1/4 cup chocolate chips

1. Preheat oven to 350° F.

2. Cream together the butter and sugar until smooth. Stir in the oil, egg, vanilla and milk and beat well. Stir the cocoa, baking powder, soda, cinnamon and flour together, then add it to the butter mixture. Stir in the zucchini and mix well. Pour the batter into a lightly greased 8-inch round or square cake pan. Smooth the top and sprinkle on the chocolate chips.

3. Bake at 350° F for about 25 minutes, or until a toothpick inserted into the centre comes out clean.

Leanne's comment:
                A 'GOURD-GEOUS' veggie disguise!

When a Recipe Calls for Sour Milk

Use 1 teaspoon of lemon juice or vinegar to sour 1 cup of milk. Sour milk can be replaced with buttermilk or buttermilk powder dissolved in water. Buttermilk powder can be purchased in bulk-food stores and should be kept in an airtight container in a cool place.

Chocolate Drizzle

Spoon 1/4 cup chocolate chips into clean, dry, heavy plastic bag. A 1-litre milk bag is perfect for this. Lay bag flat (not folded) in microwave. Microwave on Medium-low, checking every minute until chocolate is melted. Be careful not to overheat chocolate, as bag will begin to melt and chocolate will be ruined. When chocolate has melted, snip a very tiny opening in one corner of the bag. Drizzle melted chocolate through this opening as you would use a piping bag, onto the dessert in desired pattern.

Chocolate Banana Trifle

Serves 6

A terrific make-ahead dessert for a party of chocolate lovers! Keep a package of purchased jelly rolls in the freezer to make this at a moment's notice— whenever the urge for chocolate hits!

4 small chocolate jelly rolls, cut into 6 slices each
2 ripe bananas, peeled, sliced
3 cups chocolate pudding, chilled
1 cup whipping cream
2 tablespoons sugar, or to taste
2 teaspoons unsweetened cocoa
Shaved chocolate to garnish
Melted chocolate, silver decorating candies to garnish

1. Arrange jelly roll slices on bottom and halfway up sides of glass serving bowl. Arrange banana slices on jelly roll. Cover bananas and jelly roll with pudding; smooth top.

2. Whip cream until it begins to thicken. Combine sugar and cocoa in small bowl; add to cream gradually while whipping until stiff. Spread whipped cream in an even layer to completely cover all other ingredients.

3. To garnish, sprinkle top with grated chocolate. If desired, drizzle lightly with melted chocolate. For an attractive finish, top trifle with a few small silver decorating candies. Cover with plastic wrap and refrigerate for at least 1 hour to blend flavours.

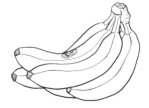

Leftover Chocolate Drizzle?

Refrigerate any leftover chocolate in bag to melt and use another time. If you keep one of these 'chocolate bags' in your refrigerator, you can enhance the appearance of the simplest dessert quickly and effortlessly.

Grilled Pineapple

Serves 6

A fabulous and simple way to end a summer barbecue, or to enjoy year-round if you have an indoor grill.

> 1 large ripe pineapple
> 2 tablespoons butter
> 1/3 cup maple syrup or honey (*omit for no-sugar version*)
> 1 tablespoon rum (*optional*) or dash cinnamon
> Vanilla ice cream or frozen yogurt

1. Keeping top intact and attached, cut pineapple lengthwise into 6 wedges.

2. In microwave or on stove top, heat butter and syrup together until butter melts. Stir in rum or cinnamon if using. Brush this mixture on all cut surfaces of pineapple. Grill until hot and nicely browned, brushing during grilling with any remaining syrup mixture. Serve hot with vanilla ice cream or frozen yogurt.

Other Fruits to Grill

Try peeled bananas, peach halves, apple or pear wedges or kebobs made from chunks of your favourite tropical or seasonal fruit. Do not overcook; the softened fruit will end up in the bottom of the barbecue rather than on your plate!

Lemon Meringues

Serves 6

Lemon curd can be made ahead and kept in the refrigerator for several weeks. Use purchased meringue shells to put this light and elegant dessert together in a hurry.

Meringues:

>   3 egg whites, at room temperature
>   1/4 teaspoon cream of tartar
>   3/4 cup sugar

1. Whip egg whites with cream of tartar until foamy. Gradually add sugar, continuing to whip until meringue is stiff and glossy.

2. Pipe or shape into 3-inch circles on parchment-lined baking sheets. Bake at 275° F for 1 hour. Turn off oven and leave meringues in oven for 1 hour more. Store in an airtight container for several weeks.

Lemon Curd:

Makes 1 1/2 cups

>   2 eggs
>   1 cup sugar
>   1/2 cup fresh lemon juice
>   3 tablespoons butter
>   2 tablespoons lemon zest

1. Whisk eggs and sugar together until smooth. Whisk in lemon juice. Add butter and zest.

2. Heat on stovetop or microwave on High 3 to 5 minutes, whisking every minute, until mixture boils and thickens. Cool; store in refrigerator.

Lemon Meringues:

    6 individual meringue shells
    1 recipe Lemon Curd
    1 cup whipping cream, whipped
    Garnishes: mint leaves, edible flowers, berries, pomegranate seeds, etc.

1. To assemble: Fold whipped cream into lemon curd. Mound onto meringue shells. Garnish with mint leaves and pomegranate seeds, flowers or fresh raspberries.

Substitution

    You may replace lemon curd with purchased lemon pie filling, if desired

Make Ahead

    Meringues can be made or purchased several days or weeks ahead. Store in an airtight container at room temperature. Do not refrigerate or freeze.
    Lemon Curd can be made up to a week ahead and stored in the refrigerator.
    The dessert can be assembled up to 1 hour ahead and refrigerated. Once the filling is placed in the meringue shell, the shell will begin to soften, so do not assemble too far in advance. Garnish just before serving.

Leanne's comment:

> *Pam put this together with a little leftover lemon curd. It's light, lemony and lovely.*

Blame It on the Weather!

If the air is very humid, it is very difficult to successfully make meringues. Wait for a day that is relatively dry for best results.

Whipping Egg Whites

You will get better volume when you bring egg whites to room temperature before whipping.

Low-Fat Strawberry Trifle

Korin Kealey, my assistant at Trillium Cooking School, suggested we make this fabulous dessert. It's a delicious low-fat way to celebrate the local strawberry season. Make it as large or as small as you like, depending on the number of diners.

Alternate layers of the following in individual parfait glasses or in a large glass serving bowl:

> Plain angel food cake, cut into bite-sized chunks
> Fresh strawberries, sliced and sweetened if desired
> Low-fat French vanilla yogurt

Garnish the top with toasted sliced almonds, mint or sweet cicely leaves, and more berries.

Maple Mousse

Serves 6

If you live in an area where sugar maple trees grow, visit a local sugar bush in the spring when the sap is running and learn how maple syrup is processed. Purchase some syrup, come home and celebrate spring with this creamy, smooth dessert.

> 4 eggs, separated
> 1 cup maple syrup
> 1/2 teaspoon vanilla
> 1 cup whipping cream
> Chocolate curls or grated chocolate

1. Beat egg yolks in heavy saucepan over low heat until light. Beat in maple syrup until well blended. Cook over low heat, stirring constantly, until mixture thickens, about 12 minutes. Remove from heat; stir in vanilla. Refrigerate until cold.

2. Whip cream until stiff. Fold in cooled syrup. Beat egg whites until stiff; fold into cream mixture.

3. Pour into sherbet glasses; freeze until firm, about 3 hours. Before serving, let stand at room temperature for a few minutes. Garnish with chocolate curls or grated chocolate.

Make Ahead

This dessert can be made and frozen up to three days ahead.

Serving Tip

Garnish pears with
Chocolate Drizzle,
page 112.

Maple Poached Pears

Serves 4

Pears can be poached in a variety of sweet liquids, from red wine to sugar syrup to cranberry juice. In my opinion, maple syrup is best.

 4 ripe pears
 2/3 cup maple syrup
 1/3 cup water
 Zest of 1/2 lemon
 1 tablespoon finely chopped pistachios

1. Pears can be peeled if desired. Leave stems on and core pears carefully from the bottom using a small spoon or melon baller.

2. In medium saucepan, combine syrup, water and zest; heat to just boiling. Place pears upright in pan. Spoon syrup mixture over. Lower heat so liquid just simmers. Cover and cook for 15 to 20 minutes, or until pears are very tender when pierced with the tip of a sharp knife. Time varies with ripeness of pears. Spoon syrup mixture over pears occasionally during cooking.

3. Remove pears from pan; refrigerate until cold.

4. Bring cooking liquid to boil; boil gently to reduce to half volume and thicken. Chill until serving time.

5. To serve, place one pear on each dessert plate. Spoon syrup over. Sprinkle with pistachios.

Strawberry Ice Cream
(without an Ice Cream Maker) Makes about 2 cups

We had lots of laughs the day we did this recipe on the show. Korin and Karen were sitting on the floor rolling the tin back and forth between them, happily reverting to their childhood days! This is a fun activity for kids of all ages, in the classroom, at camp or in your home kitchen. You will need two coffee tins with lids—one that is 13-ounce and the other a 2-pound tin.

2 cups fresh strawberries, hulled, mashed
1/3 cup sugar, or to taste
1 teaspoon lemon juice
1 cup whipping cream
Crushed ice
Coarse salt

1. In a 13-ounce (369 g) coffee tin, combine mashed berries, sugar, lemon juice and whipping cream; stir to mix well. Place plastic lid securely on tin.

2. Place filled tin inside a 2-pound (1 kg) coffee tin. Fill the space between the two tins with crushed ice and coarse salt, sprinkling a layer of salt on the ice every 2 inches. Place plastic lid securely on larger tin. Set the tin on its side. Rotate the tin constantly by rolling it on the counter or on the floor for about 15 to 20 minutes, or until ice cream is frozen. (The easiest and most fun way to do this is to have two or more children roll the tin back and forth between them.) The ice cream is ready to eat as soon as it is frozen. Be sure to wipe the salty water off of the smaller tin before removing lid.

Leanne's comment:

How you ask? Let's just say this is how Pam gets her friends frosted and giddy! Everyone feels like a conehead when they're on the floor rolling coffee cans with homemade ice cream as their goal. This is cheap, easy fun and a great flavour favour.

Index

A

B

C

D

E

Index

Index

Index

The Trillium Cooking School
www.pamcooks.com

Not your typical cooking school! Classes are held in a fully modern kitchen in Pam and Read Collacott's 160-year-old renovated log home in a picturesque setting near North Gower, Ontario, a short drive south of Ottawa.

Since 1983, Pam Collacott and a changing list of visiting chefs, cookbook authors and cooking teachers have taught hands-on and demonstration cooking classes on a wide range of topics. Classes such as the popular Friday evening "Dinner at Eight" dinner party classes are booked months, even years, in advance!

Several television series such as YTV's "Take Part", CBC's "The Great Canadian Food Show" and CTV's "CJOH News at Noon" have often filmed segments at the school.

A warm welcome awaits you at the end of the long laneway that winds through the woods to the door of the Trillium Cooking School.

We hope that you enjoy cooking with *PamCooks: Favourite Recipes From the Trillium Cooking School*.

To order additional copies of *PamCooks*:

Please send cheque or money order, payable to: Trillium Cooking School for $17.95 + 3.00 (postage and handling) + GST @ $1.47 (TOTAL $22.42) for each book to: Trillium Cooking School, R.R.#2 North Gower, ON K0A 2T0

Also available from Pam Collacott: *The Best Of New Wave Cooking*—a collection of family-friendly recipes for the microwave oven, from Pam's weekly microwave cooking column which ran in the *Ottawa Citizen* for 9 years. Timeless classics updated for the faster pace of today's family, indexed cooking tips, and conventional oven instructions for many of the recipes.

To order Please send $10.00 + 3.00 (postage and handling) + GST @ $0.91 (TOTAL $13.91) for each book to: Trillium Cooking School, R.R.#2 North Gower, ON K0A 2T0

Cheque or money order only, please, payable to: Trillium Cooking School

Be sure to indicate if you would like your books signed and personalized!

Viewers' Comments

My tastebuds went into overdrive as I watched you and Leanne on TV recently.

Helen M.

Those Sticky Buns looked "to die for."

Elizabeth S.

I use my bread maker daily but haven't been inspired to do anything different until I saw your show!

Carol S.

What I enjoy is the fact that the ideas you feature are practical as well as fun to prepare and present.

Heather D.

I enjoy your recipes. Everything always looks easy and delicious.

Claudette P.

Keep up the good work. Your recipes are a delight to my large family.

Shirley K.

I feel like your recipes for comfort food, like Turkey Shepherd's Pie are like meals from the old farm!

Donna C.

Thank you. We really enjoy your show and like how you make it seem so easy.

Marie C.

Your recipes are so good and not out-of-this-world ingredients. And you always explain them so clearly. I'm definitely a fan, though an old one (73 years old, or young!)

Ann P.

As I watched you and Leanne make soup on this bitterly cold day, I'm reminded that I've been wanting to thank you for your many fine recipes and suggestions for cutting costs and labour. I've collected and used many of them from both TV and the newspaper.

Irene B.

Keep those recipes comin'!

F. Carpenter

We enjoy our bread machine but always look for more ideas from you.

Jeanne G.

I enjoy watching you as much as you enjoy cooking. Keep up the good work.

Sue P.

What we love mostly about your recipes are the very simple basic ingredients, simple to prepare without frills, enjoyable, nutritious…

M. J. Lyons

I like your recipes because, as you say, most of the ingredients are in my cupboard.

D. Hiscath

You cook in a simple yet creative way!

Elisabeth R.

I have tried several of your recipes over the past years with great satisfaction.

J. Boileau